DIGGING UP PLUGSTREET

The Archaeology of a Great War Battlefield

For Walter.
R.O.

For my parents
And in memory of John Brown, Walter & Fred Kirk and
Dick & Jack Fisher, ancestors who all returned from the
war, and of Gunner George Bows who died in uniform.
M.B.

DIGGING UP PLUGSTREET

The Archaeology of a Great War Battlefield

Richard Osgood and Martin Brown

Published in August 2009

A catalogue record for this book is available
from the British Library

ISBN 978 1 84425 542 9

Library of Congress control no. 2009923200

Published by Haynes Publishing, Sparkford,
Yeovil, Somerset BA22 7JJ, UK

Tel: 01963 442030 Fax: 01963 440001
Int. tel: +44 1963 442030
Int. fax: +44 1963 440001
E-mail: sales@haynes.co.uk
Website: www.haynes.co.uk

Haynes North America, Inc., 861 Lawrence
Drive, Newbury Park, California 91320, USA

Design and layout by James Robertson

Printed and bound in the UK

CONTENTS

Acknowledgements

BELOW *The authors, Martin Brown and Richard Osgood, at work.*

Before work even started, a number of individuals provided huge assistance to the project: Peter Stanley, Al Palazzo and Michael Molkentin (then a summer scholar) from the Australian War Memorial, Lt-Col Mark Foxe (Australian Army), and Ian Passingham, all ensured we were fully furnished with historical background information on the Battle of Messines and the involvement of the 3rd Australian Division,

ABOVE *Conservation work in progress on the German* Pickelhaube *discovered at Plugstreet.*

and also the training that took place for the battle at the Bustard on Salisbury Plain. Lt-Cols Nigel de Foubert and Robert Steptoe were very kind in ensuring we gained access to sites on Salisbury Plain.

Putting together the project design and obtaining the necessary permissions to undertake this – the first archaeological excavation of a Great War battlefield in Wallonia – needed the assistance and support of numerous individuals. Jean Bourgeois, Dominique Loridan, Francis De Simpel, Jean-Michel Van Elslande (Comines-Warneton Historical Society) and local councillor Jean Jacques Vandenbroucke. Philippe Mignot ensured that this application process was as painless as possible. Axelle Letor and Pierre Sartieaux provided the relevant cadastral map. Peter Holton of the Commonwealth War Graves Commission (CWGC) advised us on the correct reporting procedures in the eventuality of finding human remains on site. Rob Troubelyn oversaw all elements of recovery of the Australian soldier on behalf of the Belgian Army and was of huge support in ensuring proper conservation, while the CWGC office in Ieper assisted hugely with loan of a tent for the exhumation.

The scientific assistance of Dr Andrew Shortland and Dr Patrick Degryse must also be acknowledged.

A huge area was surveyed with magnetometry by Peter Masters, whose results were essential in our siting of the excavation areas. The excavation trenches were supervised by Kirsty Nichol, Jon Price, Steve Roberts, Steve Litherland, Avril Gibson and Daniel Phillips under the EOD supervision of Rod Scott, Chris Ralling and Gontrand Callewaert. Aerial photography and cartographic work was undertaken by Birger Stichelbaut and Peter Chasseaud (the latter also being artist in residence), whilst Ian Cartwright and Eryka ('Egg') Pownall were responsible for site photography. In addition to excavating, Paola Filippucci and Nick Saunders carried out extensive anthropological studies in the area. Rob Janaway and Egon Soenen created new methodologies for conserving archaeological finds of Great War vintage. In addition to supervising the off-site finds work, logistics for the project were managed by Shirley Whitfield. This work was carried out at our excavation lodgings, the Messines Peace Village, which was a venue that met all of the project's needs splendidly.

The excellent excavation team was composed of Sylvia Agius, Graham Arkley, Bev Bailey, Carla Connolly, Adam Cooper, Henry Daniels, Nicholas De Simpel, Jane Draycott, Katherine Fennelly, Alastair Fraser, Angela Jobson, Androulla Johnson, Sue Jordan, Swantje Krause, James MacNaughton, Keith Maddison, Audrey McCready, Mat McLachlan, Michael Molkentin, Carl Ralling, Joanna Ramsay, Glen Redman, Anthony Roberts, Tori Roddy, Patrick Roelens, Justin Russell, Laura Scharding, Becki Scott, Brian Shottenkirk, Derek Smith, Chantel Summerfield, Fran Valle Ralph Whitehead and Lesley Wood.

All recorded live munitions were collected and destroyed by the DOVO later. We are also grateful to the DOVO Captain-Commandant Karla Beerens for allowing us to proceed working under this arrangement.

We were delighted to be able to guide so many visitors around the site, from local enthusiasts to those individuals engaged upon the 90th anniversary commemorative march for the start of the Battle of Passchendaele, including Major Chris Carling and Andy Robertshaw, to visitors from Australia. Included within our list of visitors were local archaeologists Johann Vandewalle, Janiek De Gryse, Marc Dewilde, Mathieu de Meyer, Frederik Demeyere, Franky Wyfels, Bert Heyvaert, and Franky Bostyn. Lt-Col Paul Smith of the Australian Army visited site with his wife

BELOW A terrain model of Messines village and environs was constructed at Cannock Chase in 1917 to assist in the training of New Zealand troops for the operation.

Wendy as guests of No-Man's-Land. Paul then represented the Australian Government at the wreath-laying service on 3 August 2007.

Bill George, Chris Maple, Ruth Pelling and Ralph Whitehead were instrumental in the production of post-excavation elements of the report writing process. Information on the Cannock Chase site and the training model appear courtesy of Ian Wykes at Staffordshire County Council.

Without the permission of the farmer M. Delrue, however, none of this project could have taken place – to him our profound thanks. Our other great duty of gratitude is to Claude and Nelly Verhaeghe of l'Auberge in Ploegsteert. In addition to their providing

our lunches and end of dig meal, they enabled our participation in the 'Last Post Ceremony' at the memorial in Ploegsteert, and introduced us to all the parties involved in the project and smoothed our way. Quite simply without Claude there would not have been an excavation and our knowledge of the archaeology of the battle of Messines would have been all the poorer.

So many individuals and organisations have given freely of their time and expertise in support of the project. We are more than grateful to everyone for their assistance as this project is very much the sum of its many parts. If we have omitted you, please accept our apologies.

Richard Osgood and Martin Brown
July 2009

Authors' note:

We have been fortunate in having a number of artists and photographers involved in this project. Anyone wishing to buy work from them should contact the artists direct:

Peter Chasseaud
Studio 3S3, Phoenix Arts Association, 10-14
Waterloo Place, Brighton, BN2 9NB, UK

Søren Hawkes
http://www.passchendaeleprints.com/index.htm

Ian Cartwright
Institute of Archaeology, 36 Beaumont Street,
Oxford, OX1 2PG, UK

Erika Pownall
eggydread@hotmail.com

In the Beginning

When one reads about battles of the First World War, the Somme, Passchendaele, Gallipoli, Jutland, and of the 'disasters' that befell the forces of Britain and the Empire, one might be forgiven for feeling amazed that the British Army actually ended on the winning side. For too long there has been a narrative that avoids discussion of the huge military successes of the war, successes indicative of good planning, good training and skilled troops. The Battle of Messines is a classic case in point. Although its objectives were in some ways limited in comparison with the campaigns mentioned above, it nonetheless was a huge victory but one which seems almost consigned to the footnotes of general histories of the conflict. This is the story of the first all-arms battle, the start of modern warfare perhaps. A battle of tanks, aircraft, a well-planned and executed artillery barrage, infantry who knew their role precisely and a culmination of the mining war: the detonation of 19 huge mines under the German front line.

An observer wrote:

Messines was not the greatest battle of the war. There were many other greater and more lasting in their gains. But Messines was unique, the first and last of its kind, and in its opening, dramatic beyond description. For the battalion, it was the first great action after months of trench life and preparation, and although all were not so hopeful of its far reaching results as those at home, there was grim satisfaction in smashing back the Hun with sheer might of arms. It could be done, and the most powerful system of defence he was able to devise was unable to resist the blow.[1]

Perhaps this victory just does not sit well with stories of generals being nothing more than 'butchers and bunglers'. No doubt we all feel we know about the story of the First World War, of soldiers being sent over the top to be machine-gunned in droves. We know of the mental images painted by the war poets, but how representative are they?

There is another story to tell: one of training and of careful planning, and one in which objectives were attained. These victories chipped away at the strength of the Central Powers and made Allied victory in 1918 possible. These facets of the First World War often go unmentioned, but without these elements of a soldier's life there could have been no victory. For the Battle of Messines, training was an essential. This is a tale we can tell through history and through archaeology.

The authors, both being archaeologists that work alongside the British Army on Salisbury Plain in Wiltshire, are familiar with the necessity for military training and the manner of its conduct. The British Army acquired its first land holdings on the Plain in 1897, as a cavalry manoeuvre area, and there has been training here ever since. As one would imagine in over 100 years of military training, a huge

OPPOSITE *The site of the Australian 3rd Division encampment on Salisbury Plain in Wiltshire, now a field covered with poppies.*

legacy of military archaeology has been left. Training features from the Boer War through to the campaigns in Iraq and Afghanistan still leave visible physical traces to a greater or lesser degree. During the First World War, there was a huge influx of soldiers onto the Plain. Soldiers from South Africa, Newfoundland, Canada, New Zealand, and from across the British Isles, were brought to this part of England. The Australians also arrived: men from Bridgetown to Bendigo, from Kangaroo Island to Kurrajong. There were farmers, timber hewers, bank clerks. All had joined to fight, both for Empire and for their country. The most famous Australian campaign of the First World War is probably that fought in the Dardanelles, Gallipoli, and yet they gained far greater success and suffered far more casualties on the Western Front.

On discussion with Dr Peter Stanley, the then Principle Historian at the Australian War Memorial, we found that one of the Australian units that had come to Salisbury Plain in the First World War fought its first battle at Messines – the Australian 3rd Division. This Division formed part of the right wing of the Allied attack on 7 June 1917, alongside the New Zealanders, as part of II Anzac Corps. From both an archaeological and historical perspective we were able to concentrate on two specific regions, two training areas that were integral to the Corps: Salisbury Plain for the Australians and Cannock Chase in Staffordshire for the New Zealanders.

Peter found an ideal summer scholar to undertake documentary research on the museum's holdings relating to the Australian 3rd Division's training on Salisbury Plain: Michael Molkentin, a historian and initial battlefield archaeology sceptic from the University of Wollongong. In studying the Australian records Michael found a rich resource – from embarkation to service records, medal rolls, postcards, letters, casualty records, inquests, satirical magazines, photographs, maps, paintings, terrain models, film from the front and even footage of King George V reviewing soldiers of the Australian 3rd Division on Salisbury Plain, complete with their shivering kangaroo mascot! In addition were the artefacts of war, souvenirs

brought back from the front. These can give a remarkable insight into the lot of the soldier and are a comparable subset of the record left by infantrymen in the ground over which they fought, artefacts which now form part of the archaeological record. The great geographic distance of Australia from Europe is also fortunate from our point of view, in that the records have escaped the destruction of bombing raids of the Second World War – a fate which befell many First World War records in Britain and Germany.

Michael looked at all the documentary resources while we concentrated on the archaeological remains, as this would give us huge information on the training regime that was to lead to the successes of Messines. He then joined us for the fieldwork side of the

project in Belgium. For the first time in an archaeological fieldwork project the research aims were to follow an army from training to theatre to establish a context for the events. What survived? Did the historical documents tally with the evidence in the soil?

Beyond our thoughts on training we wanted to see if there was any way in which we could evaluate the efficacy of training. This would only be possible if we could examine the actual trenches the Australians used, fought over, and re-fortified in their first action in theatre. We therefore had to look to Belgium, and for the first battle honour of this new Division: the Battle of Messines. It was a battle which commenced at 03:10 on 7 June 1917 with the detonation of 19 colossal mines, explosions that could be heard as far away

as England. The Australian role in the start of this battle was both as engineers who led the mining and initiated the explosion beneath Hill 60 to the north of the Messines battle front, and also as an infantry fighting force alongside the New Zealanders as II Anzac Corps on the southernmost flank of the attack.

One of the exciting facets about the project was that it was the first time an archaeological approach had been taken to research on the First World War in Wallonia.[2] The No Man's Land archaeological team had specific research aims – the intent to follow a particular unit from training to theatre being one. Our approach was described as innovative.[3] Not only was this the first excavation of a First World War site in Wallonia using an accepted wide range of archaeological techniques, but, as far as we

ABOVE *The Australian 3rd Division reviewed on Salisbury Plain by King George V.* Photograph by T. Fuller of Amesbury, courtesy of his grandson, J. Fuller

ABOVE *The remnants of Factory Farm: bonded brickwork in the spoil of the mine upcast is all that remains of this farmhouse following the explosion beneath it in 1917.*

were aware, this was the very first attempt in any period of archaeology to follow a military unit from its training through to its baptism of fire on the battlefield in an attempt to establish whether their training had indeed succeeded. Perhaps our work would also add to a current debate over revisionist approaches within First World War archaeology in that commanding officers could learn the lessons of previous, unsuccessful, campaigns and that the Allied forces were not simply 'lions led by donkeys'. This was not simply something we wished to pursue over a single small excavation trench – this was a landscape-wide project.

As with many of the best-laid battle plans, our research design really did not survive first contact! It soon became apparent that we were dealing with a far greater project. The First World War did not occur in a landscape akin to a blank canvas. The St Yvon region in Belgium had survived as later-medieval landscape until the huge devastation wrought by the fighting. Moated farms, hedgerows, and field systems

were all to disappear. Whole communities were displaced and had to re-order their world on their return. The story of the Ploegsteert area must include the lives of Belgians both before and after the war if one is to contextualise the conflict zone and tell the complete story.

Ploegsteert wood, or 'Plugstreet' to the Tommies, was familiar to many soldiers in the war, as most regiments spent some time here. Anthony Eden, Winston Churchill and Roland Leighton had all walked in the wood – the latter even featuring it in his famous poem 'Villanelle', written to Vera Brittain. It was the location for many strange primitive 'houses' or shelters for troops; it was also a thoroughfare for Australian soldiers moving to the front line on the morning of 7 June – the trees holding German gas fired into the wood like mist on an Autumn morning meant that many of the Australians never left the wood. Just to the north of the wood is the small hamlet of St Yvon. This was the attack front for the 33rd Battalion of the Australian 3rd Division and so the focus for our archaeological attention.

Soon we will lose our last contact with veterans of the First World War; we are on the edges of living memory. At the time of writing there is just one surviving British veteran of the trench warfare of France and Belgium – Harry Patch, a man who served with the Duke of Cornwall's Light Infantry.

It is also only in recent years that archaeology has been considered worthwhile as an exercise to gain a greater understanding of the First World War. This is our story of the archaeology of just one battlefield of the time, of the training that occurred beforehand, of the effects this had on the local population in Wallonia and the landscape they knew. As archaeology is about people, ours is also a story of the soldiers who fought and died in the war, and how they made their lives bearable.

By way of introduction to the project, Michael Molkentin, the Australian historian with the project, describes his reasons for becoming one of those converts.

'As a military historian and, I must admit, self confessed "archives junkie", it is probably not surprising that I approached the Ploegsteert Project with a somewhat large measure of scepticism. I mean, why would anyone need

to dig in the dirt to understand the role that Australian soldiers played in a battle here 90 years ago? Doesn't the paper – the endless reams of war diaries, reports, maps, soldiers' letters and diaries and oral history – tell us all we need to, and indeed, can possibly hope to know about the past? As an Australian, as far as I was concerned, archaeology's useful application only began where the documents finished; say, for example, in the study of ancient Indigenous peoples.

'My involvement with a battlefield archaeology project was entirely serendipitous. In 2004 the Australian War Memorial (AWM) awarded me a scholarship to write a history of the Australian 3rd Division's training at Salisbury Plain in 1916. It was part of a collaborative project between the AWM and the UK Ministry of Defence, whose archaeologists were planning to excavate an Australian training site. The research turned up some interesting evidence about training and raised a bunch of questions for future research. The archaeology

on the other hand raised a few interesting points, but as far as I could tell it wasn't groundbreaking. However, the whole exercise was enough to pique my curiosity, not the least because I suddenly realised that there were serious academics and institutions out there (not just TV shows) that thought there was something in this battlefield archaeology stuff.

'A second scholarship (from the NSW Premier) allowed me to explore things further. I received a grant to go to Europe to observe NML's excavation at Ploegsteert, as my proposal said, "to evaluate the potential of archaeology in teaching and learning Australian military history". It would be my first trip to the battlefields – an exciting enough proposition after years of devoted study – and I could certainly see the value of visiting a site. As with most Australian military historians, my work is heavily influenced by Charles (C.E.W.) Bean, Australia's First World War official historian and founder of the AWM. In 1919, Bean set a tradition among Australian historians by

ABOVE LEFT *Harry Patch was the last surviving Tommy to have fought in the trenches on the Western Front. He died in 2009 at the age of 111.* Jonathan Falconer

ABOVE *Historian Michael Molkentin in an Australian trench in the lip of Ultimo Crater.* Ian Cartwright

ABOVE *The excavation team walking to site, past the edge of Ultimo Crater. This image was taken with a plate camera and its composition draws inspiration from a photograph of a gun limber by Frank Hurley.* Ian Cartwright

RIGHT *The entrance to Toronto Avenue cemetery – last resting place of many Australian troops including 33rd Battalion soldiers.*

conducting a systematic study of the Gallipoli battlefields, to solve, what he dubbed "the riddles of Anzac". Among these were details relating to the Turkish side of the campaign and its chaotic (and poorly documented) early days. Although not an archaeologist himself, Bean "based his approach on the methodology of Oxford historian R. G. Collingwood" who had studied Hadrian's Wall. Ultimately, his fieldwork shed new light on the military aspects of the campaign (such as revealing how far the first Diggers made it before being cut off), identified unburied dead and collected relics for the Australian War Memorial. Australia's most prominent historians have, ever since, been visiting battlefields as part of their research. Yet few, if any, I sceptically acknowledged, had travelled with a shovel.

'I spent my first couple of days in Europe in my boxy little hire car (which would soon earn the nickname "the Mark IV"), picking my way across Australia's famous battlefield and cemetery sites. Why Bean and so many others had come to these sites was immediately clear. There is something profoundly poignant, albeit well outside of the pragmatism of academic research, about walking across a battlefield and then stopping in a cemetery to see the results of it all. At the same time, though it was a frustrating and even destabilising experience. The peaceful green pastures on Pozières Ridge for example, and the pristine uniformity of the headstones tucked away in its folds, belied the images in my head – images scratched out by soldiers in their diaries and letters of grotesque and corrupt landscapes and mountains of dead.

'And still, there in the landscape, my academic understanding grew as pondered the gap between the verdant fields before me, and the soldier's accounts and photographs in my backpack. I have, for example, long been able to recite the respective ranges of different weapons of the day, but suddenly in the flat featureless Flemish countryside, they became significant. Terrain, which had previously been contour lines on a trench map, suddenly became a key source to understanding how battles unfolded.

'Arriving at Messines Ridge, after months of reading in the archives, suddenly brought the battle into a fresh focus. Of course, I knew in my head from the documents that Messines was a key tactical position because of the observation prowess it gave the enemy. Standing below the ridge, as so many Australian and New Zealanders did in the dawn of 7 June 1917, I could for the first time feel why this was a tactically important objective. Could it, perhaps, even have been worth the cost in human life? This, of course, is an unsettling question that all historians of the First World War confront, and indeed, a question that becomes all the more unsettling when one is standing on the old German front line in Messines Ridge Cemetery, surrounded by the battle's victims. For it is here that tactical requirements and human suffering – ends and means, head and heart – come charging at each other with fixed bayonets.

'And I didn't suspect it, but things were not about to get easier at the excavation site.

'Firstly, to my surprise, I didn't see a single shovel for the first two days at Factory Farm. The geophysicists surveyed the site while Richard Osgood and I wandered around discussing the terrain and comparing it with some trench maps. The ground answered at least one question immediately – why did II Army's staff officers select this site as the right hinge of the entire attack – was it just random or was there a rhyme to their reason? The edge of the advance sat in a slightly elevated paddock; not enough to draw the historians eye when viewing a map, but certainly enough to stop bullets from enemy units beyond the battle zone when you are standing in no-man's-land just to its north. For staff officers who, according to the folklore, never went forward to look at the ground, this was quite a clever piece of planning.

'Trudging around the paddocks with Richard, it suddenly occurred to me that what's above the ground is as important to an archaeologist as what is beneath it. A fence, terrain feature or shop flogging off battlefield tours is as pertinent to the archaeologist as a bullet, bomb or tin of bully beef in the dirt.

'This much broader definition of what constitutes archaeological evidence led to a second revelation about battlefield archaeology. Living in, walking around, eating from and talking to locals in this place reminded me of something that I knew, but never really appreciated about these battlefields. Their history as combat zones is very brief – just four years. Their history as feudal farming communities, post-war reconstruction zones and battlefield tourism destinations, on the other hand, stretch into centuries. All manner of artefacts pointed to this in my first few days at the site, and they ranged from the medieval bowl that was excavated on the first day to the electric fences that the landowner had erected, supposedly in response to the burgeoning battlefield tourism industry. As the dig went on, the site probably revealed more about the post-war Belgians than it did about the 'diggers and Huns' that fought here in 1917. The excavation of a German pillbox, systematically destroyed after the war and raided for its valuable iron supports was a fascinating insight (and, I think, the beginning of a whole new field of study) into the hardships of the people who tried to live here in the 1920s. The hordes of 'trench art' (much of it post war, as Nicholas Saunders reminds us in his excellent book) in and around Ypres, and the industry for 'battlefield relics' also taps into this otherwise hidden history that is overshadowed by the war itself. Archaeology was, in fact, expanding my understanding of this sites' significance and reminding me afresh that for every grieving mother in Australia there were thousands of Belgian and French peasants who had to rebuild their entire communities following 1918.

'In the midst of the excavation I took a few days to visit other archaeological sites around the old Ypres salient. Here I had my third revelation – conflict archaeology (as I was now calling it following revelation No. 2) is not just an academic exercise. For ordinary battlefield tourists it communicates an evocative sense of the past to people who like me, struggled to reconcile the past and present of these sites. Like many tourists and school children, with excitement I explored an excavated German trench system at Bayernwald and a reconstruction (based on excavation) of the dugouts beneath Zonnebeke church. I walked along the 'Road to Passchendaele'– an excellent example of archaeology's value in communicating the past to tourists – guided through a series of small excavations and interpretive panels. As a teacher, I was particularly impressed by how these sites taught the past by linking it with the present.

'At the end of the "Road to Passchendaele", I came upon an excavated section of the Zonnebeke–Roulers railway line in a cutting just next to Tyne Cott Cemetery. There were, strangely I thought, flowers and wreathes scattered among the sleepers. The interpretive panel explained that here during excavations, archaeologists had discovered the remains of a Lancashire Fusilier. People had, I realised, turned this excavation into an informal site of commemoration. A rusted set of train tracks – a twisted, century-old relic with little aesthetic historical importance – had become the focus of people's attempts to, as I had been trying to, come to terms with this war.

'Conflict archaeology, I have concluded, is not just about digging up battlefields in the quest to revise military history's existing narrative. It encompasses a comprehensive study of war's broad and varied landscape: combat, culture, home fronts, commemoration and above all, the individual human (not just soldiers', generals' and politicians') experience of war. It is overwhelmingly 'social' and 'public' in its approach, being both about ordinary individuals and for ordinary individuals – the tourist, the school student and the television audience. By opening up and interpreting the landscape of conflict, archaeologists have provided a new focus for commemoration, tourism and education while forcing us historians to confront a new type of evidence and dozens of new areas, outside of the battlefield, to explore.

'With few veterans of the twentieth century's defining conflicts left, it is likely that the role played by archaeologists will only grow in importance. Few others are equipped to make the landscapes and items they hold speak to us like the witnesses to history that they are.'
Eryka Pownall

BELOW *A cross of sacrifice in one of the many cemeteries of the Western Front.*

CHAPTER 1

From Moats to Mines

Battlefields are the product of brief moments of human activity. Even the sites of the First World War, where fighting could rage for months over the same ground, are the product of relatively brief activity in the long life of a landscape, and it is worth considering how that landscape looked prior to the arrival of the armies, and whether topographic features shaped the Front in the study area.

Although there is archaeological evidence of prehistoric and Roman activity around St Yvon, the principal shaping of the landscape seems have taken place in the Middle Ages. Even today the low-lying, flat lands of Flanders are scattered with moated sites, some still occupied by their farmsteads. Moats are a typical feature of the medieval landscape both in England and Belgium.

The landscape features around the moats were also physical: early maps of the Comines–Warneton show the moats sitting among strip fields and closes, orchards and stands of woodland, with occasional larger woods, such as Ploegsteert Wood itself. Some sites are depicted on 16th-century maps, and the patterns of landscape continue from this period through the 18th and 19th centuries, so that the landscape of 1914 was essentially a later-medieval one. It was into this landscape that the armies of 1914 marched. They were not the first soldiers here; they followed Burgundians and Englishmen during the Hundred Years War, as well as Marlborough and Louis XIV's men, and the soldiers of Napoleon and Wellington.

Flanders had been the cockpit of Europe for centuries. Unfortunately these men would not be the last here either; one surface find from the fields surrounding the site was a Second World War German 9mm pistol cartridge.

Fields of Conflict

The landscape in our study area is still more wooded and has a more intimate feel than the countryside to the north of Ypres, due to the smaller fields and the lines of trees that sometimes border them. If anything, the maps of the landscape prior to the war suggest that this somewhat enclosed feel was even more prevalent then. This landscape was ideal for skirmishing, with troops taking cover behind field boundaries, and in the drainage ditches that ran beside roads and in the woodlands. However, flat ground, open where there were no trees, remained difficult to assault in the face of accurate musketry and machine-gun fire.

Initially the Allies held much of the high ground including Messines, Hill 63 and Ploegsteert Wood. German attacks in late 1914 drove them from the Messines Ridge and, for a time, threatened Ypres itself, but as both sides drew breath after the mad months of marching and fighting since the outbreak of war, the line settled down and the soldiers began to create the Western Front as we imagine it: rifle pits were connected and deepened, ditches were deepened and improved by the creation

OPPOSITE *A wooden cross erected by the 'Khaki Chums' at St Yvon, in the field of the best documented episode of the Christmas Truce. The football has been left as a later offering, presumably on tales of matches in no-man's-land over this cease-fire period.* Eryka Pownall

of traverses, and buildings were fortified as trenches and strongpoints were strung across the landscape. Then the first strings of barbed wire were stretched in front of the trenches to impede enemy advances. At St Yvon the British had been taking cover in sunken-lane sections, behind the embanked road and in ditches dug and built to create fortifications, while they used Plugstreet Wood (as it had become known to the soldiers who couldn't manage the local pronunciation) as a garrison and a reserve area where troops could be assembled, fed, held in reserve, and all hidden from the eyes of German airmen. Observers were also positioned in the Château de la Hutte on Hill 63, looking over the wood toward the enemy line and the occupied land beyond. Meanwhile, the Germans set about fortifying Wytschaete and Messines in order to dominate the ground

below, and digging in on the higher ground before St Yvon. Where the ground fell away southwards toward Armentieres and Warneton, they occupied the abandoned farm that they named '*Wasser Gut*' after its moat, and which the British came to know as Factory Farm. From the moated site the Germans could see toward the enemy in front of them and to the south. The rise of the ground obscured views northwards but it did mean that some attackers moving across no-man's-land would be skylined on the crest of the low ridge, presenting excellent targets. The farm would have been an artillery target, as aerial photographs show, but remains on the site, such as girders, reveal that the Germans reinforced the buildings, creating bunkers behind the brick façades. The farm, with its fine views and fields of fire, was too good a position to relinquish.

Goodwill to Men

By Christmas 1914 both sides were entrenched, both literally and metaphorically, in the landscape. Neither side was ready to attempt another assault, while the cold weather reduced further the will to do much more than survive. Clearly the war would not be over by Christmas, as the popular press had predicted, but without respite and reserves it could not progress, and reinforcements were not yet trained for the Front. In this breathing space occurred one of the most remarkable and famous moments in military history.

The story of the 1914 Christmas Truce is well known. On the night of the 24th German carols were heard from the enemy trenches and were responded to by the Allies. By Christmas morning there were unofficial truces in operation at various locations along the line, depending on the mood of troops and their officers. Souvenirs, food and drink were all exchanged and, famously, there was at least one international football match in no-man's-land. One of the locations where a truce is known to have taken place is within the study area. A classic account comes from Lieutenant Bruce Bairnsfather, famous as the artist who created Old Bill, the evocation of the grumpy old soldier who grumbled his way to victory. Bairnsfather's letters and sketches record meeting 'Fritz' and 'Henrich' in a turnip field a few hundred yards north of our excavation area. Here the 1st Battalion of the Warwickshire Regiment emerged from their trenches to meet their opponents. Archaeologically, such a meeting is unlikely to leave any traces, but in terms of the popular perception of the landscape the truce remains a significant event, marked by a small memorial erected by re-enactors from the Khaki Chums, and commemorated by pilgrims who specifically travel to see where this iconic event took place.

BELOW *The Christmas Truce 1914: German soldiers of the 134th Saxon Regiment photographed with men of the Royal Warwickshire Regiment in No Man's Land on the Western Front.* Imperial War Museum (IWM) HU35801

We're Here Because . . .

With Christmas over, the two sides resumed hostilities. During 1915, although the Germans continued to push against the British, things calmed down enough to be euphemistically known as a 'quiet' sector. While the Ypres salient became a byword for dangerous conditions and ever-present threats from the enemy, at Plugstreet both sides used the trenches as areas where troops could experience the Front for the first time or be rested after a tour in a hotter' sector, such as the salient. On the surface, at least, all seemed quiet. The Germans were happy to sit on the higher ground; while across the line the British knew that to attack the Messines Ridge – which was key to any assault in this area due to its commanding position – without careful preparation, was madness. Nevertheless, the reverse S-curve of the line, bowing eastwards around Ypres and back westwards along the Messines Ridge, caused problems for the British defenders of Ypres. The German salient south of Ypres meant that the southern flank of British positions was always vulnerable and guns could be ranged into the rear area of the Ypres Salient. Meanwhile the German occupation of the Ridge gave them an advantage in terrain, allowing them to observe the British lines and reserve areas and seek out targets for their artillery. Finally, at a basic level, Belgium had to be liberated, by as much force as was necessary. For the Germans, possession of enemy territory was effectively winning. They could afford to allow the Allies to batter themselves against their defences. Accordingly, the Germans continued to improve their defences; not just the trenches, but the thickets of barbed wire and, as their strategy of defence evolved, the construction of concrete shelters along the lines. Today, the visitors to the Bayernwald near Wytschaete can visit reconstructed trenches and see such shelters. They were not pillboxes with embrasures for rifles and machine guns; rather they were intended to provide cover for soldiers, often in ground unsuitable for dugouts. Unlike dugouts these shelters also meant that the defenders were very close to their positions if an attack came.

Once More unto the Breach

To assault the well-prepared Germans, an equally well-prepared attack plan would be needed. The British commander in Belgium was General Herbert Plumer. On first sight Plumer was the archetypal British general, an ageing, rotund, heavily mustachioed man, who would later become the model for David Low's caricature Colonel Blimp, who appeared in cartoons in the 1930s and 1940s. He apparently epitomised the sort of general beloved of the 'lions led by donkeys' school of military history, but this could not be further from the truth. Plumer was a careful, steady general and one who understood perfectly that he was not fighting battles but was actually engaged in a massive siege. Messines, as Basil Liddell Hart wrote, was the best example of how to correctly fight a siege war. Sieges were not won by lightning strikes but by careful preparation, by making breaches in the enemy

BELOW *The reconstructed German trench at Bayernwald. The hurdle revetment is a modern replica of typical German trench-building methods.*
Eryka Pownall.

fortification; by taking the breaches, biting into the enemy line, holding it and expanding outwards from it. Whether one fought for Alexander, Caesar, Henry V or Wellington, sieges were broken by breach and by mining. Whether at Badajoz in Spain, Petersburg in America, or even at Jericho with Joshua, fortifications were breached by bringing down the enemy line. Before the introduction of explosives this was done by mining under the enemy and collapsing the tunnel beneath the walls, but later mines were used to blow breaches in either walls or trench lines. Plumer realised that this was the tactic to utilise if he was to crack the Messines Ridge and set his Royal Engineers to tunnelling. Tunnelling would take a year. Meanwhile, mines were only part of the plan, as the breaches they made had to be taken. In operations in 1915 at Loos and on the Somme in 1916 the British had not been successful at capturing mines and forcing the breaches. Plumer needed well-trained men to be able to follow up the shock and awe of the initial blasts.

ABOVE *Field Marshal Sir Douglas Haig (centre front) with his Army commanders at Cambrai. From left to right behind him: General Sir Herbert Plumer (2nd Army), General Sir Julian Byng (3rd Army), General Sir William Birdwood (5th Army), and General Sir Henry Horne (1st Army), with other senior officers.* IWM Q9689

LEFT *Tunnellers place sacks full of explosives at the head of an excavated tunnel. The officer on the left is using a geophone to listen for signs of enemy mining activity.* IWM Q115

CHAPTER 2

Making Soldiers

In 1914 the British Army stood at somewhere near its present level of 100,000 men; they garrisoned the Empire on which the 'sun never set'. Reinforced at home by Territorials and abroad by Dominion troops such as the Indian Army, they were still small compared to the conscript armies of Germany and France. Weakened in the early battles such as Mons and Le Cateau, the Tommies had held the Germans but were in a poor state to resist them on the Western Front in a prolonged series of campaigns. Lord Kitchener, as Secretary of State for War, realised that this new European war would not be a short encounter like the 1870–71 Franco-Prussian conflict and endorsed a massive recruiting campaign. His efforts, coupled with patriotic fervour that sent men in their thousands to recruiting offices in the late summer and autumn of 1914 led to a massive expansion of the British Army. The initial target had been for another 100,000 men, but the numbers soon far exceeded this, approaching one million men eager to be involved in momentous events before the war ended in what was seen as the inevitable defeat of the Kaiser.

These men came from all walks of civilian life, but they were just that, civilians; most had no experience of military discipline save for learning to march in organisations such as the Boy Scouts or the Boys' Brigade. The exceptions to this were recruits from Ulster and southern Ireland, where paramilitary activity had been rife in the early years of the century in the face of agitation surrounding Home Rule debates. Nevertheless, these Irish volunteers were still not fully made soldiers, much less the miners, tram-drivers and clerks who flocked to the recruiting offices in those heady, early days of the war.

The Roman military theoretician Vegetius wrote much on the subject of training. He stated two key points regarding recruits: the first was that a small number of trained men could resist a much larger force of untrained troops and defeat them, while the second was that to send untrained troops into battle was tantamount to throwing them away and effectively murdering them.[1] Although writing centuries before the age of machine gun and heavy artillery his words still acted as a *vade mecum* to the classically trained officers of the Army of 1914. It was clear to Kitchener and his staff that the 'Old Contemptibles' had held the German onslaught because they were well trained, professional soldiers who could rattle off aimed rifle fire at such a rate that the Germans had overestimated the number of machine guns opposing them. However, he also knew that to turn the mass of men now at his disposal into useful soldiers would be no mean feat, since the Army infrastructure was not geared up to such a dramatic expansion.

Across the country Army camps sprouted like mushrooms, at first temporary, using bell tents and marquees, but then, as the weather worsened and the Army was able to organise labour, becoming semi-permanent as wooden

OPPOSITE Number 22430 Gunner (later Driver) Walter Osgood of the 8th Field Artillery Brigade, Australian 3rd Division, grandfather of co-author Richard Osgood.

GENERAL VIEW of BUSTARD CAMP. SALISBURY PLAIN.   PHOTO BY, T L. FULLER. AMESBURY.

ABOVE *The first encampment near the Bustard, prior to the digging of training trenches.* Photograph by T. Fuller of Amesbury and courtesy of his grandson, J. Fuller

RIGHT *The site of the Australian 3rd Division encampment on Salisbury Plain in Wiltshire.*

hutments were built to accommodate the New Armies. On Salisbury Plain, a British Army training area since 1897, new barracks sprang up at Larkhill, Codford and Durrington, while a railway spur was built to bring men, supplies and equipment from Salisbury north to the rolling chalk of the training area.

On Cannock Chase in Staffordshire the story was the same, although here the Army leased land from Lord Lichfield, drawing on a tradition of using the area for summer manoeuvres. The scale of this deployment was, however, quite different from the Victorian field days, as two camps, each big enough for a division was built, again with its own railway line, known to all as the Tackeroo Express, after nearby mine works.

At Blandford Forum in Dorset shipless sailors arrived to form the Royal Naval divisions, including a junior officer and poet called Rupert Brooke. On the Ashdown Forest in Sussex, later to become A.A. Milne's *Hundred Acre Wood*, and high on both Dartmoor and Otterburn the Royal Artillery practised their gunnery. Near Marlow in Buckinghamshire, the Guards

marched out to practise defending a road junction and valley, and everywhere men dug. When it was not Kipling's 'Boots, boots, boots' it was spades and shovels. On chalk, gravels, sands and clays, and even on the granite cliffs of Pembrokeshire, men learned to dig. The whole landscape was being militarised. For example, an Imperial War Museum photograph shows troops constructing a timber bridge, while in the background networks of trenches sprawl across the hillside behind a row of civilian houses.[2]

The 1908 *Field Fortification Manual* incorporated the lessons of the Boer War, where trenches had not been adequate against the accurate Mauser rifles of the Boers, but it also distilled lessons learned during observation of the Russo-Japanese War in 1906, when trenches, machine guns and artillery had been very much in evidence. The diagrams and plates clearly show that far from being unprepared for the impending conflict there were those in the High Command who had anticipated the nature of the coming European

BELOW *Lining the old pack way by Larkhill, these huts were home to the soldiers of the Australian 3rd Division in 1916. None of the buildings in what must have been a bustling shanty town now remain.* Photograph by T. Fuller of Amesbury and courtesy of his grandson, J. Fuller

Lark Hill and Durrington Camps, Salisbury Plain

hostilities. Perhaps they were not prepared for the scale of entrenchments, from Belgium to Switzerland, nor for the duration of this phase of the war, but they had foreseen the importance of getting men into cover in the earth, away from the sweep of the Maxim gun and the range of shells delivered by the gunners.

Meanwhile, at the Front, the race to the sea ended and as the last German attacks faltered each side drew respite and dug in to face each other across no-man's-land. As soon as they were in position both sides began to fortify and improve their trenches. Reports from theatre ensured that digging would become an essential part of every man's training. Yet it was not tactical direction alone that made trenches spread across a landscape far from the war. Military expediency also had its part to play. While some of the men who volunteered were fit, strong members of the industrial working class, many more were from the burgeoning white-collar jobs in offices, banks, town halls, post offices and other similar employments. They were neither strong nor used to outdoor work. Members of the urban poor, driven as much by desire for wages and food as much as by patriotism, were similarly not immediate material for an army. Both needed to be shaped and strengthened for what was to come.

Unfortunately the rush of recruits had not only put strains on the provision of barracks. Uniforms, boots and equipment were also in short supply, but there were plenty of tools to be had; men could drill until they were able to move like soldiers, and could march, even if in their own boots, until they were footsore, but still mobile. Even so, they needed further training to build esprit de corps, team-working, fitness and stamina.

They also needed to learn how to dig. In particular the Pioneer Battalions raised at the end of 1914 had skills to learn in this area. The training manuals of 1914 estimated six months for the training of soldiers, and defined what should happen when there simply was not the infrastructure to support it and training became a good deal more haphazard; in consequence of which retired officers and NCOs returned to the ranks to aid the war effort. Some were

natural trainers, others were still Empire soldiers, teaching methods more suited to India or South Africa than to Flanders; even so the recruits laid the foundations of the Army that would beat the Germans. The old methods of advancing across open country in waves supported by accurate rifle fire were all well and good and served the men of the very early war well. Unfortunately by Christmas 1914 when trench warfare was the world the recruits would enter, new skills were required. Fortunately, the recruits were keen to learn and men already in the line were equally keen to pass on their new-found skills. Pamphlets and articles on the situation poured from the Front, and the Army was supportive of their spread among the new officers and as an organisation was catching up with the situation in both training and equipment, an example of the latter being the 1914 leather webbing that at least allowed men to become familiar with their kit. By 1916 the training camps and their Training Battalions were running efficiently and turning out proper soldiers.

Erskine Williams was called to the colours in March 1916. He was a musician and had joined the Army in 1915 under the Derby Scheme, named after Lord Derby, Kitchener's successor as Secretary of State for War, which allowed men to volunteer for their chosen arm of service and to be called when required. He had volunteered as a bandsman but underwent the same basic training as all his comrades-in-arms. Williams was sent to Brocton Camp on Cannock Chase to the 12th (Training) Battalion of the Nottinghamshire and Derbyshire Regiment, better known as the Sherwood Foresters. In a series of illustrated letters and postcards to his family he described his new life. He left a remarkable picture of basic training in the middle of the war, including bayonet and bombing (grenade) practice, marching and use of the rifle, both on the static range and in practising the short rushes and firing that could still be useful in the advance if the German trenches were breached. Part of this drill included advancing on the range, firing as they went, before jumping into trenches and firing at the targets. Meanwhile, photographs of the Chase show assault courses with low barbed-wire entanglements beneath which the men had to crawl without getting snagged. Williams also drew his comrades practising wiring using the pig-tailed screw pickets, effectively giant corkscrews that allowed barbed wire to be erected or repaired without the need for the noisy banging in of fence posts that would attract German fire in a dark no-man's-land. The networks of trenches still visible on the Chase also show how much digging the men did.

Digging, wiring and bombing were all skills essential to trench warfare. Williams also dealt with the essentials of life, writing at some length about food, both rations and the cakes and fruit, including a rare pineapple sent from London. On one occasion he even sketched the bacon, eggs, bread and tea given to the men for breakfast.[3] The importance of food has been underlined by material found in excavations on the Chase and at Plugstreet, as we will see.

From Little Billabong to Larkhill

It was into this world that the Australian 3rd Division arrived early in 1916. By this time training had progressed from its rather ad hoc beginnings. The Division was posted to Larkhill on Salisbury Plain, occupying barracks on the Packway, the main street connecting the new camps. Unlike some soldiers of the 2nd Division who had assumed training in practice trenches at Broadmeadows, Melbourne, the men of the 3rd Division had only experience of drill, parades, and route marches. Some had been lucky enough to undertake an element of musketry practice – for the 43rd Battalion in dry river beds of the Sturt River, and practice attacks in extended order in Bendigo for the 38th Battalion[4] – but it was a wholly new experience for these men to gain field experience.

BELOW *Soldiers of the Australian 2nd Division inside a typical barrack hut of the Great War period.*

ABOVE *Australian soldiers on parade in the market square of Market Lavington, co-author Martin Brown's home village in Wiltshire.* Photograph by T. Fuller of Amesbury and courtesy of his grandson, J. Fuller

OPPOSITE TOP *Ye Old Bustard Inn was well known to Australian Army soldiers camped at nearby Larkhill.* Captain A.W. McMillan/AWM H13866

OPPOSITE BOTTOM *The Bustard Inn today. Very little has changed since the original photograph was taken.*

In addition, some of the problems that had dogged the New Armies were still present. On arrival in Wiltshire there was a marked shortage in weaponry and ammunition for these men; photographs taken during training show a mixture of Short Magazine Lee Enfield (SMLE), the rifle of the British Army, and long Lee Enfield, which had been replaced by the SMLE some years before. As well, although they had received some training, the Australian War Memorial includes documents that discussed the various shortcomings of the soldiers in the early stages of their time in Britain and found that 'Bayonet training was an area in which the Third Division needed particular attention. Australian bayonet training had been superseded by a new standard, developed by the British bayonet school at Aldershot. . . . Rather than rushing ahead individually, men practised the principal of control by advancing in squad formations, in good order against straw filled dummies.'[5] From images taken of the 3rd Division Pioneer Corps at Larkhill, one might dispute the realism of this training – perhaps even questioning the effectiveness of the work in the practice

trenches at the Bustard Inn. This, however, may simply reflect an 'informal' use of a set of demonstration practice trenches dug next to the barrack huts.

There is evidence that men were inspired by their training, presumably discussing their experiences of the exercises back at their barracks in some detail. There could, though, be tragic consequences when this training was too inspirational. Private Charles Edward Sargentson of the 39th Battalion (Service No 1405) was a farmer from Stawell, Victoria. He joined the Australian army on 3 April 1916 and was killed in a bayonet accident in his barracks on Salisbury Plain on 6 November of that year. The inquest decided that he had died in Fargo military hospital due to injuries sustained to his abdomen as a result of 'skylarking'. Back at camp a few of the men had continued the lessons they had learned, when a scabbard was dislodged from one of the bayonets attached to a Lee Enfield rifle; this wasn't noticed as it was dark in the hut. In the ensuing shenanigans Sargentson was stabbed by Private Thomas Williams and died. He was 38 and left a wife – Mrs Lena

Sargentson, and daughter, Nancy. Lena's heart-wrenching letters are still to be found in the National Archives of Australia with desperate queries addressed to the Australian authorities to check whether it was indeed her Charles that had been killed, after the wrong service number (1406) had been given. Sadly this was nothing more than a clerical error and her husband was indeed dead.

The inventory of his personal effects is interesting when one considers material one might find in the remains of a trench on an excavation. The panoply consisted of: one identity disc, one handkerchief, a pair of gloves, a badge, a cigarette case, two knives, two razors, a purse, a comb, a shaving brush, and a musketry book.

BELOW *The grave of Charles Edward Sargentson at Durrington cemetery. Charles, an infantryman in the 3rd Division, was killed in a bayonet accident during his training on Salisbury Plain.*

Charles Sargentson was buried at Durrington Cemetery on Salisbury Plain. The tragedy of the matter was that use of the bayonet was a relatively minor part of warfare on the Western Front: Richard Holmes, in his book *Tommy*, reveals that of a sample of 200,000 British casualties, only 0.32 per cent were inflicted by bayonet. This was something that was predicted by the historian of the 37th Battalion of the Australian Imperial Force (AIF) who felt that, at the front, the bayonet would be of more use as a toasting fork than a deadly weapon.[6] Meanwhile, Siegfried Sassoon, writing of his training in France, recalled 'a massive, sandy-haired Highland Major', speaking 'with homicidal eloquence' on the ' Spirit of the Bayonet'. Sassoon felt that they were expected 'to jab the life out of the Germans' but his tone suggests that he was not convinced.

While bayonets were not often used, and seem to have been the cause of very small numbers of injuries, the troops of Australian 3rd Division seem to have made extensive use of them during the Messines offensive, particularly during their attack in front of St Yvon. The use of bayonets is illustrated, if one reads between the lines, in the 33rd Battalion War Diary when discussing prisoners – or the lack of them – taken during the assault:

> *Enemy's Morale . . . Very few showed any fight and there was no attempt anywhere to make a determined stand. They would not face the bayonet, and cringed for mercy. Their morale could hardly be lower.*
> *Casualties inflicted: It is a conservative estimate to say that 150 were killed in the Battalion Area. These were accounted for by our Artillery and a large percentage by the bayonet, the remainder by rifle fire, bombs and rifle grenades. Very few bombs were used and only against dug-outs. Rifles were used only when personal contact could not be obtained.*
> *Captures: We took three prisoners: they were Red Cross men and unarmed.*

This last line is telling – with all of the Germans apparently putting up little resistance and surrendering in droves, the fight having been knocked out of them, it is significant that only three prisoners were taken by the Battalion, and these 'Red Cross men'. Is it possible that the visceral reality of close combat, with bayonet and bomb, rendered the likelihood of German defenders being able to claim quarter less liable, or is there some truth to stories that the Australian 3rd Division had heard rumours of the maltreatment of Allied prisoners of war and its men were thus less inclined to mercy? Admittedly the Anzacs were angry at having been gassed and lost comrades on their way up through Plugstreet Wood, and the 'heat of the moment' could be offered as mitigating circumstances, but the lack of prisoners taken, despite the 'cringing for mercy' does suggest what today might be called a war crime. To debate such things nearly a century after the fact is futile but it reveals the true face of warfare.

In addition to bayonet training and instruction on musketry (including firing one's rifle while wearing a gas mask), the men of the 3rd Division were lectured on range-finding, care of firearms and ammunition, and scouting. All this came alongside the inevitable lot of the infantryman – long route marches, often in full kit. By far the most important lesson these men would learn, however, would be how to live and fight on the Western Front. Not so much the brigade-level movements over open country in the fields towards Stonehenge, but rather how to live in the front-line trenches which they would face on moving to France or Belgium.

BELOW Larkhill, 5 August 1916. Members of the 3rd Pioneer Battalion, AIF, are trained in bayonet fighting. C. Wadeson/ AWM H16986

Despite some of the apparent shortcoming and accidents and the prescriptions of the War Office, the Australian commander, General Monash, had some distinct ideas of his own. They included definite views on the digging of trenches, promulgated to the General Staff in August 1916: 'Promiscuous digging teaches very little and spoils the ground for other work.'[7] He was, of course, correct. By 1916 the Western Front and the training grounds had been extensively dug over – both real and simulated battlefields were covered in existing trenches. For individual units to make new works would have little value; better to work with what already existed, as would be the case in theatre, where the Anzacs would not be digging new trenches but would be called on to reinforce, repair and adapt trenches.

Out on the Plain they learned to create Lewis-gun positions and to create dugouts, some of this under fire to add an air of authenticity. They also had to learn field craft that would serve them in open country. While they were not going to learn how to replicate the 7ft-deep fortifications prescribed in the manuals, they were taught how to dig in when in no-man's-land or in open country. One of the new soldiers wrote home: 'We had to lie flat down on the ground for two hours digging with a small entrenching tool until we had a big enough hole for each one to kneel in and then we had to start with the pick and shovel to make them into right trenches. It was pouring all the time. . . .'[8] These were localised entrenchments, sometimes dug under fire and called shell scrapes, and even today infantrymen on Salisbury Plain learn this essential skill.

However, the existing trench systems were not ignored. Monash also believed that his training regime should be as realistic as possible, including occupation of trenches for days and nights at a time and the practice of trench routine, including relief and supply. These exercises gave the opportunity to learn from mistakes, including such as Harold Gazzard's experience of getting lost for several hours one night in trenches near Orcheston. They also gave men chances to encounter at least some of the realities of soldiering:

Rain swept the open country and poured into the white-chalk trenches. When at night several companies entered the trenches to take up their positions, men floundered through pools of whitewash, and got covered with sticky white mud. Verey lights went hissing up through the driving rain, to illuminate a dreary landscape. Rifles cracked, and the dull detonations of hand grenades momentarily drowned the angry hissing of the rain.[9]

The evocative picture could be Flanders but in fact describes Salisbury Plain.

The practice trenches that were so wet and slippery lay to the north of the Bustard Inn situated between Larkhill and Shrewton. Although now filled in they can still be seen from the air, and faint depressions on the ground marks their line. Unusually there is a 1:5,000 scale trench map for this set of features, akin to those which are so familiar for the main battlegrounds of the war. Alongside a 'German' front line, the map denotes names for individual 'Allied' stretches of the training feature: 'Comb Alley', 'Queer Street', 'The Haymarket' and others. While this might appear a random set of names, there was method even here for these replicated names of trenches from the Bois Grenier sector of the Western Front, and referred to 'the Australian

occupation of this sector in early 1916 and their action at Fromelles in July of that year'[10]. One additional detail is present on this trench map, at first glance something that looks insignificant: a small spider-like feature that extends beyond the great web of the trench network. Yet it is this feature that is crucial to the whole story of the 3rd Division, its training and its role in the First World War, for this illustrates a mine crater, one that has been refortified by attacking units.

The trenches were part of Monash's great plan for this Division, for them to experience live fire and also to live in similar conditions to the Western Front for days at a time before being relieved by other units. Field dressing, communications, trench raiding, and all aspects of logistics were to be accomplished too. An extant photograph shows men of the 3rd Division sitting in what must be the front line of this set of practice trenches – appearing to have been posed for a visiting photographer, perhaps to illustrate the active role of the Australian forces – before the actual trench system had been completed, as the men are still far from protected by trench or parapet.

Michael Molkentin's research led him to the belief that:

many of the recruits perceived their first tour in the Bustard line as a novel experience. Typical was the practice of addressing letters written during exercises as from 'in a dugout'; or as John Baillie quipped to his sweetheart, 'You can now say we have been "in the trenches". Try this on your dad for a joke.' Others were swept up in the feeling of excitement and adventure conveyed by such a realistic training environment. Twenty-seven-year-old Harold Peters sent his family 'a few lines written from the trenches, where we have dug, fought, slid, swam, splashed, and been soaked through and through, and still enjoy the joke'. Still, others were simply struck by the oddity of living for days below the surface. Thom Britton, a station hand from rural New South Wales, described it as 'highly amusing' to watch the grotesque positions that comrades fell asleep in. Of further amusement to Britton were the crudities of trench life. He observed

men scavenge food from the bottoms of their boots and attempt to shave in canteen water.[11]

What was equally important in these exercises was the use of live ammunition, for only this can truly give the soldier an appreciation of his weapons, their potential and their danger. Lieutenant Vincent Callen, who would be killed in action on 20 August 1918, wrote a letter describing the use of live rounds at the Bustard:

We have had the most like the real thing since we left. Bodies split up into sentries, entrenchers and firing parties with a friendly 'enemy' ever on the alert to catch

H. 29

us napping. Then we had an attack nearly 'fair dinkum'. The aeroplanes cruised round and got our signals. Then they raced back to the artillery behind us, gave them the range and they started a 'barrage' with live shells . . . this barrage is a tremendous shelling of the enemy trenches with shrapnel, high explosive, and other shells, causing them to seek the safety of their dug-outs. Our troops go over the parapet to within 30 yard to where the shells are bursting and wait there. At a given signal the 'barrage' is lifted ie fire ceased and we rush the trenches and settle what's left of the foe. It was very interesting work, but the rain made things pretty rotten and it was very cold at night.[12]

If familiar with the fact that Allied units practised in training trenches before being moved to theatre – after all there are numerous surviving examples in Britain – perhaps the detail of practice involved in training for specific attacks might come as a surprise. It might even go some way to dispel the theory that the infantry were 'lions led by donkeys', sent by unthinking staff officers to inevitable death on a mission with no chance of success. Specific battles were often trained for in the minutest detail and Messines is a case in point. The training of the unit which would fight in Belgium in 1917 as II Anzac Corps, meant that these troops were, by 7 June 1917, fully aware of their roles, their method of fighting, and their objectives. The New Zealanders practised

BELOW *Soldiers from New Zealand training in Britain. The terrain suggests that this is Salisbury Plain, which was used by New Zealanders who were based at Sling Camp. The date is 1916 or later, given the helmets being worn.*

N.Z. TROOPS TRAINING.

hard for this battle at Cannock Chase. On Salisbury Plain, the Australian 3rd Division also prepared carefully for the coming of their first major campaign of the First World War.

Not only was this unit inculcated in the niceties of generic trench warfare, they were ready to experience entering the maelstrom created by the explosions of huge mines beneath their opponents. The experience of exploding mines, of fortifying the resulting craters and 'turning round' the German front line once captured were essential lessons and ones which made a huge impression on those involved. According to Pedersen, the climax came on 6 November when four artillery batteries, signallers, engineers and four aircraft supported an 'assault' by five battalions:

> *A large mine [of 5000lb (2,2270kg) of gun cotton] was exploded under the 'enemy' trenches, the infantry rushing the crater as the barrage formed a protective box around it. Men blocked the communication trenches as Lewis gun teams co-operated with bombers on either flank to cover the wiring parties consolidating the position.[13]*

The crater left by this mine, fired by a Captain A. Tootell resulted in a crater some 30ft deep and 8ft across.[14]

As an artillery war, a successful battle depended on the close cooperation of the guns with the infantry, on the accuracy of target spotting and ranging. The level of detailed planning required to achieve success in the confusing circumstances of battle was impressive, and this was in part corroborated by the satirical magazine of one of the Field Artillery Brigades involved in the practice:

> *Tues 6 Nov: At 8am (just after daybreak) when the guns came up, communications had already been tried. . . . The scheme was for the infantry to attack the enemy trenches (distant not many yards from our own) and at precise prearranged times, they were to be assisted by barrages of artillery fire. Engineers, Flying Corps, Trench Mortars and Army Medical Corps all cooperating. At 9:45am, artillery opened fire. 10:00 (zero time), a mine in*

> *enemy territory was exploded, the crater of which becoming part of the infantry's objective. The artillery commenced the first barrage, or curtain of fire, at 10:01, and this was kept up for 3 minutes. The second barrage commenced at 10:04, continuing until the Infantry had taken, and were entrenched in the crater of the mine. The taking of the crater proved a difficult task, for the Infantry had to call upon the Artillery for extra fire by means of the SOS signal, distinguished by the discharge of a rocket. The experience produced a clear comprehension of the obvious necessity for absolute accuracy in the control of fire, and to the onlooker was a very vivid picture of what actual trench warfare is like, more particularly in regard to the Infantry; for after having taken the crater they had to dig themselves in, and this, even with the shovel is no light task in the hard chalky substance. Nevertheless, with the entrenching tools they appeared to make light work of it, and soon were properly entrenched in the crater.[15]*

Digging Trenches

The Australian records are replete with detail, but what traces would remain on the ground? The Army Training Area of Salisbury Plain has many trench systems of the First World War pattern scattered across it. These have been identified by a mixture of aerial photography and field survey and included on both the Wiltshire and Defence Estates databases of archaeological sites. Some are visible as earthworks, still zigzagging across the landscape, others are long back-filled, levelled and grassed over. Although no longer evident on the ground, these trenches are visible from the air when ground conditions are right. They can also be shown using geophysical survey.

Most trenches do not have particular units or exercises associated with them. At Shipton Bellinger trenches are known to have been used for experiments by the Royal Engineers in dealing with barbed wire, and close to the Bustard Inn the Australians are known to have carried out the exercises described above.

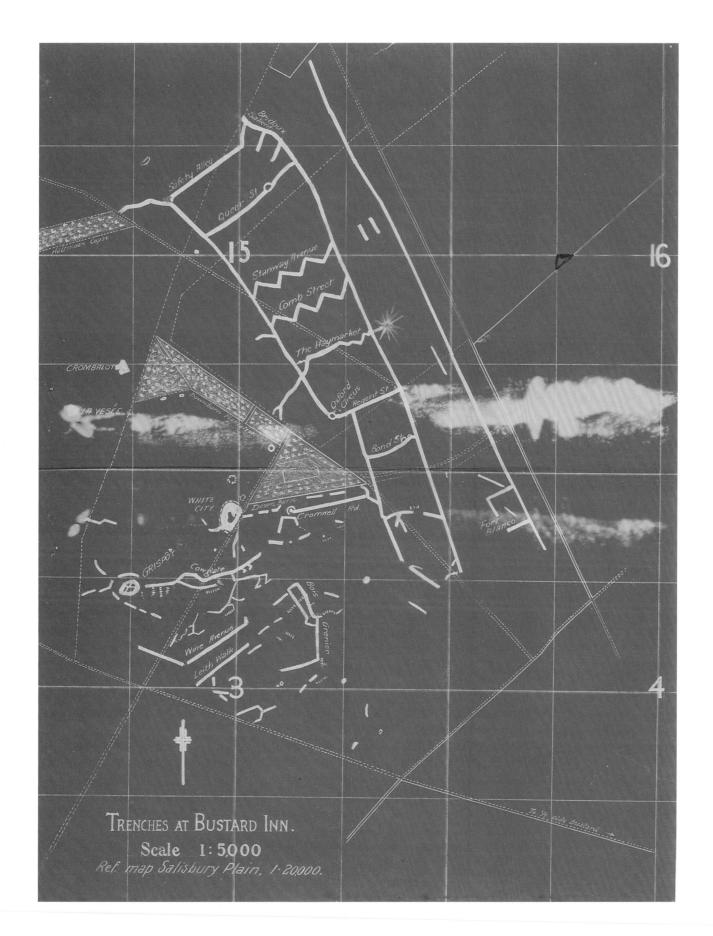

TRENCHES AT BUSTARD INN.

Scale   1 : 5000

Ref. map Salisbury Plain, 1 · 20,000.

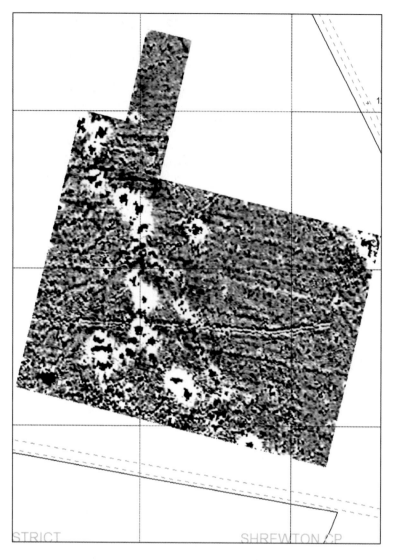

STRICT   SHREWTON CP

ABOVE *Aerial photograph of the Bustard practice trenches on Salisbury Plain taken by the pioneer of British air photography of archaeology, O.G.S. Crawford in the 1920s. Note that many of the trenches to the north of the image have already been filled in. The mine crater is visible to the top right of the photograph and the copse of trees at the bottom is Half Moon Copse - location of many arborglyphs.* Courtesy of English Heritage. NMR SU0847

ABOVE *Fluxgate gradiometer survey of the Bustard practice trenches. The front line trenches are very clear, running from top left to bottom right/ middle. A small mine crater is also visible to the right of the front line (second square down middle column).* Peter Masters, Cranfield University

However, the archaeological remains had never been investigated. The remains are within an area still used by troops in training and this could have had an impact on them, as vehicles cross the area and troops are able to dig their own modern trenches; digging-in is still a useful skill that can save lives when bullets are flying. The Defence Estates archaeologists, working with the No Man's Land archaeological team, decided to investigate the trenches to see what survived and what the condition of the monument was. Following a resistivity survey by a group from Bristol, a number of archaeological trenches were dug across the military fieldworks.

The results of this first round of works showed the trenches did not conform to the patterns shown in the manuals, as in some

places they were only about 1m deep. The reason for this was that at about this depth the soldiers had encountered lower chalk, which is remarkably hard. This accounts for the Fuller picture of a group of men lining a trench with their rifles at the ready. The upper bodies of all the men are exposed; in addition the trench appears too narrow to have a fire step on which they could be standing. The photograph suggests that the men had also met with this denser chalk and made the best of a bad job. One thing the photo does show is that their training was good: the parados – the earth bank behind the trench – stands above head height, meaning that their heads would not be skylined, presenting easy targets for enemy snipers.

Meanwhile, the finds recovered from the

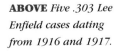

LEFT A 1917-dated Mark VII .303 Lee Enfield bullet case found in excavations at the Bustard. The date is significant in that it was after the departure of the Australians, indicating the use of the training feature by later units.

LEFT The crimped end of a blank .303 Lee Enfield round (dated 1914) illustrating that 'dry' training also took place here.

ABOVE Five .303 Lee Enfield cases dating from 1916 and 1917.

LEFT The burster tube and pusher plate from a shrapnel shell excavated at the Bustard that indicates use of artillery on site.

BELOW Some of the many First World War Australian graves at Durrington cemetery. Although the majority fell to disease and illness, two were killed in training accidents.

dig told their own story of training. A series of fired .303 cartridges, both blank and live, were recovered dating between 1914 and 1917. The date range of these rounds and the different types suggest that the ground had been used for exercises throughout the war for troops at different stages in their training. This underlines Monash's diktat that it was better for troops to practise in pre-existing trenches than to dig new works, when there were systems ready for use and adaptation. However, the area had not just been used for infantry training. The discovery of a burster tube from a shrapnel shell suggested that the trenches had also been used as an artillery target at some point, unless this was evidence of a shell that had fallen short during a live-fire exercise. Training could be dangerous – one Australian was killed by Lewis-gun fire during training, and lies in the Durrington Military Cemetery.

No traces of the men spending days and nights in the trenches practising trench routines were found, though the tins for food were absent, but it may be that, as today, troops were required to clean up after their use of a training feature. Certainly the Bustard trenches were partly backfilled shortly after the end of the war, so it may be that men waiting for demob, especially the Anzacs awaiting passage home, were employed to clean up the area. This was underlined during later excavations carried out in partnership with Bristol University, when no finds, save a prehistoric

worked flint, one of the many found on Salisbury Plain, were unearthed. However the Bristol dig did find some deeper, wider trenches toward the north of the system. Here the hard chalk seemed to have dipped away as the folds of the downland rolled northwards and the soldiers had been able to dig trenches over 1m in depth, which made them just deep enough to provide some sort of head cover once the spoil had been mounded up into parapet and parados. The trenches might not have been deep enough where German snipers were active but to give the sense of depth and an appropriate environment in which to practise movement and trench life they sufficed.

Evidence of the recruits practising a number of techniques was evident in the polished, stained chalk that indicated where boards had been laid so that men could walk through the trenches and get used to the semi-subterranean

world they were to inhabit on the front line. However, one aspect of life in Flanders for which the Anzacs could not train was the soil conditions – the infamous clinging, wet mud of the Front. In order to deal with the wet conditions A-frames were used. These timber frames resembled an inverted A; the legs helped support the sides of the trench, while the horizontal bar was both a bracer and acted as a joist onto which the boards were laid. The boards provided more secure footing for men moving along the trenches, while the gap between the bar and the trench floor was intended to form a sort of gutter, allowing liquid mud to run off toward a sump.

Unfortunately for the Anzacs the ground of Salisbury Plain, while very similar to that of the Somme, with its rolling chalk, is completely different to the heavy clays of Flanders that are, by turns, waterlogged in wet weather

Dear Old Silly. "AND WHERE DO YOU TWO COME FROM?"
Wounded Australian. "WE'RE ANZACS, MADAM."
Dear Old Silly. "REALLY? HOW DELIGHTFUL! AND DO YOU BOTH BELONG TO THE SAME TRIBE?"

or concrete hard after periods of prolonged sunshine. As a result the soldiers arrived at the Front without having practised the construction and use of these invaluable pieces of trench architecture. However, as the creation of the Lewis saps at the Ultimo crater was to show, they had learned something of this skill by 7 June 1917, as their Pioneers used the 'short reveting frame' to help hold back the loose soils of the crater lip. While the success of the men at St Yvon can be attributed to good training, clearly their time on Salisbury Plain was unable to equip them for every eventuality.

What Tribe are You from?

The Australian recruits were kept busy in preparation for their deployment but it is clear that they did not spend all their time in combat

training, and even then there were apparently long periods of waiting for something to happen.

Close to the Bustard Inn trenches is a stand of beech trees. The bark of beeches is perfect for carving and a stroll through the woods shows that men have wiled away the hours here with a pen knife – handily issued to each man – while waiting for orders. The trees include names and even addresses of men from Britain, America, and Australia, including Alexander Todd and Clyde Henry Walker of the Anzac 3rd Division.

Todd was traced from his initials 'A.T.' in conjunction to the associated carved elements of Vic, 10 AIF and 'Orbost'. This man was Service No 398, Lance Corporal Alexander Todd of the 38th AIF (10th Brigade, 3rd Division), a labourer from Orbost, Victoria. Alexander was wounded in the shoulder on 7 June at the Battle of Messines. He was later to

ABOVE *A cartoon from* Punch *magazine in the Great War, showing how the presence of Dominion troops in the UK had entered popular culture.*

BELOW LEFT *The service record of Alexander James Todd, 38th Battalion, AIF.* National Archives of Australia: B2455, TODD ALEXANDER JOHN

BELOW RIGHT *The 'arborglyph' left by Todd in Half Moon Copse on Salisbury Plain, adjacent to the Bustard trenches.*

be awarded the Military Medal before dying of wounds on 3 October 1918 after a shell hit his dugout. Some of his comrades complained that they should not have been in this dugout; they had been held up waiting for the Americans to join their advance in front of the Hindenburg Line. Alexander Todd lies in Doingt Communal Cemetery extension in France. The embarkation records, nominal rolls, and service records for Alexander Todd are all visible online[16] in the records of the National Archives of Australia and through the Australian War Memorial.

The inventory of his effects is interesting in that it indicates the sorts of artefacts that one might find on excavations of the Western Front of sites used by the soldiers. The items, forwarded to his mother, were: letters, photos, one foreign coin, one tobacco box, one pocket knife, one wallet, three coins valued at *3d* and 20 centimes, and two discs. His pay book was forwarded to AIF headquarters in London. Such items are both intriguing and potentially informative should they be found together in association with the remains of a soldier on the battlefield or in a makeshift grave.

The carving of names represents a period of boredom but may also be seen in a wider frame. Were these men seeking to assert and

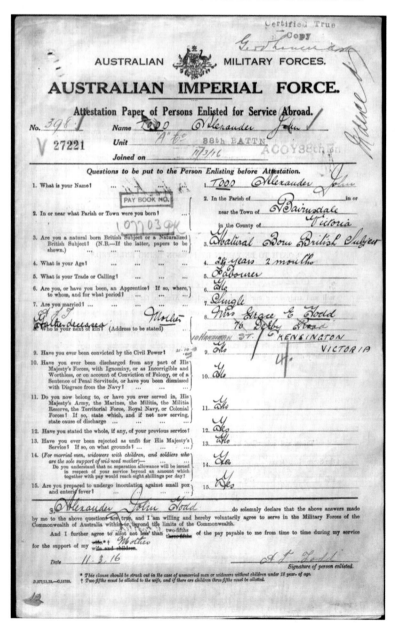

affirm their identities, to remind themselves, and us, that they were more than another number in the serried khaki ranks? That they also inscribed place-names suggests that they wanted to mark their journey across the globe and perhaps to comment on the fact that they had come to what may have seemed like one of the bleakest and most tedious places on earth!

Further attempts at retaining individuality included appearance. Within the narrow confines of Army dress there is archaeological evidence that at least some of the men were determined still to cut a dash. Many of the Australians were housed in Rollestone Camp on Salisbury Plain, where material from a rubbish dump included a bottle for Anzora. Research showed this to be an Australian hair tonic, so popular with the troops that it was advertised in the *Anzac Bulletin*, the Divisional newspaper, in January 1918. Not only was this a cosmetic product, it was also viola scented. This may be at variance with the rough and ready 'ocker' image of the Anzac, but it does

reveal that some of them were determined to look (and smell) good, probably for the ladies!

Perhaps the Australians, with their higher pay than the British and their foreign accents, were appealing but they also acquired a reputation for wildness that has passed into folklore – such as the dumping of the Codford prostitute into a well. Despite this, village tales in Market Lavington, on the north edge of the Plain, suggest that they were not so feared as the Canadians: the postmaster is said not to have minded the Anzacs, but a rumour that the

ABOVE *The January 1916 issue of the* Anzac Bulletin *with its advert for Anzora, a viola-scented hair tonic.*

LEFT *Remnants of the Anzora bottle from the Bustard trenches. Other similar bottles were recovered from the mine crater blown as part of the specific Bustard training for Messines.*

ABOVE *A map of Australia carved into the chalk of the Wiltshire hills at Fovant. This was dug close to the Australian base of Hurdcott Camp.*

LEFT *The 'rising sun' badge of Australia (right) at Fovant in 1920 ...*

BELOW *... and the 'rising sun' badge today – now a protected monument.*

Canadians were coming was enough to make him send his wife and daughters away to stay with family elsewhere.

Indeed, the Anzac forays into Lavington do seem to have been good-natured affairs, as they paraded to 'show the flag' to the natives. Photographs still held in the village museum record a parade in the market place, including the pipe band and officers on horses. Such interaction seems to have been common: *Punch*, that mirror to so much of Britain's modern history, included a cartoon of a behatted old lady addressing two Australians, marked as such by their slouch hats. She asks who they are and on being told they are Anzacs she politely enquires 'And what tribe are you from?' The visitors clearly made their mark on the landscape, trees and in popular culture! Meanwhile, the Australian view of Salisbury Plain is neatly summed up in the 1916 Christmas number of *The Yandoo*: 'Somewhere in Larkhill':

6am. 'By cripes Bill, its blanky cold! That the reveille? I've been playing the bones since about 4am ' 'Come on Joe, the quarter call's gone.' 'Orlright Bill, wait till I get my boots on. Cripes this here Pommyland will be the death of me. D— the Kaiser: they ought to put him here instead of on St Helena. Instead of fighting for a confounded, cold, clammy, cow of a country like this they ought to give it to the Germans.'

The World in Miniature

Meanwhile, not only training was generic. The blowing and fortifying of the mine suggests that instruction was being geared towards actual operational requirements. Today this is known as MRX, or Mission Rehearsal Exercise and provides excellent training for men. This sort of grounding continued until days before the attack at Messines.

At Petit Pont a large-scale model of the Messines battlefield was created for both officers and men to inspect, so that they might see how they fitted into the wider scheme and what the terrain and defences

ABOVE *Belgium, 6 June 1917. Australians of the 13th Brigade study the large contour map near Petit Pont, Belgium, which was specially made to give the troops an appreciation of the Messines battlefield. The operation, which opened the next morning, was completely successful. It was considered as much a triumph of methodical planning and organisation as it was a great feat of arms. (The men in slouch hats are of D Company, 14th Battalion.)* AWM E00632

LEFT *Remains of the terrain model of Messines made by men of the New Zealand Rifle Brigade at their training camp on Cannock Chase.*

LEFT, TOP *The foundations of one of the Australian huts on the edge of the Packway at Larkhill, excavated by the Stonehenge Riverside Project.*

LEFT, MIDDLE *The Cannock Chase Messines terrain model, with Brigade HQ and barrack hutments in the background.*

LEFT, BOTTOM *Co-author Martin Brown records the excavated section of the Messines model following its re-discovery by local archaeologists.*

they might encounter looked like. They were constructed using maps and up-to-date aerial photographs to create accurate representation of the ground. Such models of individual objectives were common, but this was unusual in that it depicted a large area of operations. Unfortunately, modern-day enquiries among the farming community in Belgium suggested that the site had returned to agriculture and been ploughed, meaning that no archaeological traces of the model would remain. However a representation of one part of the battlefield does still survive and has been partly excavated. Recent fieldwork by Birmingham Archaeology and the No Man's Land team on Cannock Chase in Staffordshire (UK) has revealed and recorded a model of the village of Messines and its defences. This model sits in the middle of what was once the New Zealand Rifle Brigade training camp. It is remarkable in that unlike the examples seen on photographs in theatre it is constructed using cement to create the terrain and trenches, while pebbles have been used to lay roads, and bricks have been employed to indicate buildings, which were given roofs. The church tower even had a pocket watch fixed on it. Research by local historians has suggested that it was built after the capture of the Messines Ridge by the New Zealand Rifle Brigade. The date of manufacture suggests that this was not a tool for MRX, but had a multiplicity of meanings. The model could be used to teach new drafts how Messines had been taken, effectively becoming a miniature battlefield tour, but it could also act as a trophy, representing a major action and significant battle honour where honour and decorations, including a Victoria Cross, had been won. As such the model not only helped train men but also embodied brigade ethos, helping to instil unit pride and build esprit de corps, showing not only what had been achieved but also what the recruits were expected to emulate. To the training drafts, even after their formal lecture at the model it remained a constant and permanent reminder at the heart of their camp. It appears also to have been visible from the German Prisoner of War camp, so may also have had other messages for the captured foe.

Realities in Conflict

Any army seeks authenticity in its training. Since Roman times the quality of training has been seen as the key to success. Today, the British Army has facilities that resemble the theatres in which they operate, sometimes peopled with 'locals' who come from the area of deployment; it is possible to look at the remains of trenches, see German-style pillboxes from Normandy, Northern Ireland watchtowers, and villages resembling northern Germany, where the Warsaw Pact was to have been fought. One can see the history of major British deployments over 90 years. All simulations strive for realism, whether in the accuracy of architecture or in details such as graffiti, while today special effects (explosions, fire, sounds) add further levels of stress to the trainee, preparing him for the front line. Yet in a real sense all these features remain only as simulacra, models of the world into which the warrior will enter. At one basic level no one is shooting at him. While there may be explosions, live ammunition and the noise and confusion of combat, the enemy, whether represented by other troops, or merely – as it was at the Bustard – by a trench line, are not firing back. While it is possible to be killed in training. this is not a regular occurrence and the likelihood is much less than in theatre.

Practice trenches of the First World War presented a remarkable opportunity for recruits to learn the skills of soldiering and to become effective, functioning bodies of troops. Nevertheless, however much Salisbury Plain resembled the Somme, nothing could prepare men either for the immediate presence of an enemy who might be so close that you could smell him cooking breakfast, or for the random, sudden deaths as distant artillery decided to drop a few shells onto 'Tommy' in order to wear down his nerves. Nor indeed would any amount of war gaming anticipate the barrage and the mine explosions that were the overture to the 3rd Division assault on 7 June. Whatever else it was like it would bear scanty resemblance to their time on the Plain.

Yet training anticipates the stresses of combat. A Royal Marine officer, talking about training on Dartmoor today, said that the worse the weather the better, because if men left for theatre able to get on with their jobs in any conditions, then they should have learned how to function should trouble occur – in effect the training aims for everything that is not out of the ordinary to come as natural to the recruit.

The same was true of the instruction given to the Australians, and to the rest of the British Army in the First World War: men were supposed to gain a foundation that would allow them to function effectively, almost unconsciously, while thinking about their specific circumstances. While the reality of training and the reality of combat were worlds apart, the skills of one supported the survival of the other.

Nevertheless, the training grounds, models and war games could only be seen as representations of reality. Complete authenticity could not be achieved with no enemy present. However, as training moved from the home nations toward the Front it became more authentic – the enemy guns could be heard, and could even deliver occasional shells and resultant casualties – but still, only the experience of actual combat would test its effectiveness.

1 Vegetius: I.9.
2 MacDonald, 1993: pl 29.
3 Jones, 1992: 3–31.
4 Palazzo, 2002: 13–14).
5 Molkentin, 2005: 19.
6 McNicoll, 1936: 21.
7 Monash papers 3DRL/2316: series 3, folder 42.
8 McFarlane letter, 26 August 1916: AWM Private Record, 1 DRL/436).
9 Fairey, 1920: 7.
10 Chasseaud, 2006: 207.
11 Molkentin, 2006: 48–9.
12 Callen letter, 13 October 1916: AWM Private Record, 1 DRL/0179.
13 Pedersen, 2007: 222.
14 See Palazzo, 2002: 19–20.
15 7th Field Artillery Brigade, *The Yandoo*, 1916: 42.
16 <http://www.awm.gov.au/cms_images/1DRL428/00035/1DRL428-00035-2760107.pdf>.

CHAPTER 3

Shock and Awe – 1917 Style

The massive movement of men and materiel made it impossible to hide preparations for an attack during the First World War. Trains, column of troops and the organisation of supply dumps and hospitals made the movement visible to aerial reconnaissance, but the Germans were not prepared for the opening move planned by Plumer. They were busy reinforcing their garrisons on the night of 7 June in anticipation of the coming onslaught, confident of their preparations and strong fortifications. However they had no inkling of the coming storm. *Oberleutnant* Engen Reitinger of the 3rd Battalion, 17 Bavarian Infantry, recorded his experiences:

> *In the front line the relief was in full swing when suddenly at 4am there was an almighty roar and the earth began to quake and everything flew off the chairs [in the blockhouse]: both officers and men poured out of the entrance into the open air. An awe-inspiring sight met their eyes. The hills from Wijtshate to Messines were enveloped in a great sea of flames. Fourteen fiery volcanoes and masses of earth erupted vertically into the air colouring it bright red. Then the great masses of earth crashed back down.*[1]

All along the German line the story was the same, mines dug deeply and in secret had tunnelled out from the Allied line beneath their enemies, and huge quantities of high explosive

had been placed in chambers ready to wreak havoc and to disorientate and demoralise any survivors. Mines were nothing new in this conflict, having been used at Loos and on the Somme to devastating effect before – as the famous film clip from the documentary of the Somme of the detonation of the Hawthorn mine and craters that still survive in the landscape demonstrates – but they had never been used before on such a massive scale; their use, and the artillery firestorm which followed, prefigured the 'shock and awe' tactic visited upon the Iraqi people at the outset of the Second Gulf War in 2003. An anonymous British member of 250 Tunnelling Company recalled the event:

> *Suddenly all hell broke loose. It was indescribable. In the pale light it appeared as if the whole enemy line had begun to dance, then one after another, huge tongues of flame shot hundreds of feet into the air, followed by dense columns of smoke, which flattened out at the top like gigantic mushrooms. . . . The whole scene was magnificent in its awfulness. At the same moment, every gun opened up, the din became deafening and then nothing could be seen of the front, but the bursting of our barrage and the distress flares of the enemy.*[2]

The desired effect was clearly achieved, as *Leutnant der Reserve* Kohl reported:

OPPOSITE *Factory Farm crater in 2007, with the excavation team behind it.* Ian Cartwright

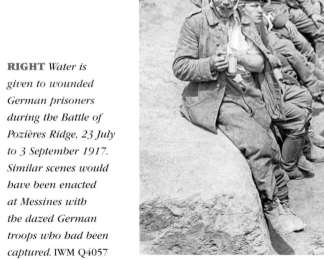

The fields around looked like an endless chessboard covered with overlapping craters. . . . Everywhere I bumped into stragglers . . . leaderless and wandering like lost sheep from a scattered herd. . . . At the Barbarahof I came across a Saxon Leutnant who had obviously suffered a nervous breakdown.[3]

Meanwhile, on Hill 60, another objective of the attack, the devastation of both the trenches and the defenders was marked: 'Hell on Earth. . . Trenches were squeezed together so quickly and thoroughly that enemy dead were seen in a standing position. Relatively few prisoners were captured from Hill 60 proper, and those of the enemy who were alive were nervous wrecks, a great number of them actually crying with fear.'[4]

Army interrogation of German prisoners later showed that the rippling effect of the mines detonating north to south down a ten-mile section of the line spread panic as one after another blast came and no one knew where the next would strike. The result was a breakdown of morale and some panic. The German front was devastated and its troops either buried, torn apart or mentally shattered. However, the front line was not the extent of the defences and as the shock wore off and realisation of the attack registered, defence was organised – some of it surprisingly quickly – and in some areas German resistance intensified. Yet this reaction also showed the depth of the front line, where artillery, reserves and some machine guns were sufficiently far back from the explosions not to have suffered the worst trauma, either physical or mental, so reducing disruption to organisation and morale.

The Messines attack had been long in both planning and preparation. For two years the Messines Ridge had been a problem for the Allies, dominating the landscape and providing fine observation and defensive positions for the German Army. A frontal assault could prove a bloodbath for the Allies unless an innovative approach to the assault was conceived. Mines were deemed to be the answer. Although the use of mines had a long pedigree in bringing down walls, extending back to the Middle Ages, and had been used against entrenchments in the American Civil and Russo-Japanese wars, the First World War saw them come to prominence in a conflict

OPPOSITE *Zero minus 10 minutes on 1 July 1916. The mine under Hawthorn Redoubt is fired before the assault at Beaumont Hamel on the Somme. The photographer is about a mile from the blast. Some 45,000lb of Ammonal has exploded causing a crater 130ft across by 58ft deep. It would have been a sight like this at Messines in the early morning of 7 June 1917. IWM Q754*

LEFT *Larkhill, 5 August 1916. Three members of the 3rd Pioneer Battalion, AIF, dig a trench. From the left they are Privates Jeannette, Chamberlain and Petroski. AWM H16987*

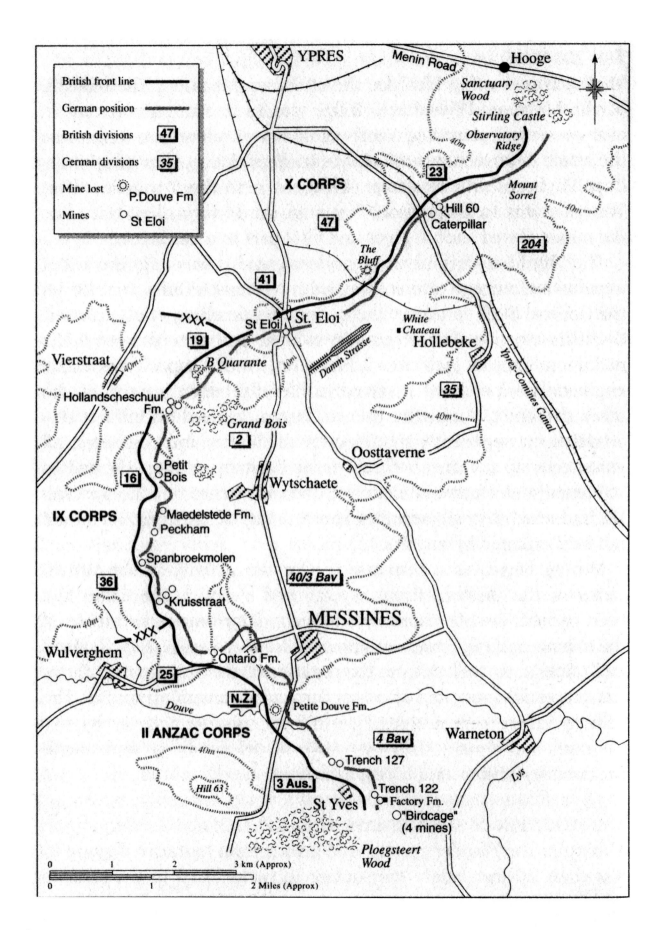

that can be regarded as a siege on an international scale.

It was John Norton-Griffiths who convinced the General Staff that mining on a major scale could be used to do more than make breaches in the enemy lines. To effect his plans specialist tunnellers were recruited from mining communities and the labourers who had dug the tunnels for the expansion of the London's sewer and Underground networks. This latter group were particularly useful in Flanders, where the clays were similar to some of the soils encountered under London. They developed a system of working using a frame that enabled the man at the face to use both feet to dig the spade into the clay before him. The method coined their name: the 'clay kickers'. Behind the kicker was a chain of men putting the soil into sandbags, removing it down the mine gallery and then hoisting it up the shaft to the surface. Even then the spoil did not cease its journey. The thick clay of Flanders may have been good for digging but, having a distinct blue-grey colour – by contrast to the brown of the surface soils – dumping quantities of this distinctive material close to the mines would alert enemy aerial reconnaissance fliers to mining activity. If this occurred, the enemy would try to collapse the mine entrance with artillery, but they would also launch countermines – (galleries sunk to try to locate the Allied excavations)

and either blow explosive charges – known as camouflet mines – adjacent to them and collapse the gallery, entombing their opponents, or breaking through to engage them in short, sharp actions fought hand-to-hand in the dark depths, like something from the works of Tolkien. Nevertheless, the Tunnelling Companies from Britain, Canada, New Zealand and Australia persevered, driving ever eastwards toward the enemy positions.

Opposite the Germans garrisoning Factory Farm was the 3rd Canadian Tunnelling Company. From a position just behind the British front line they sank their shaft some 70ft deep and dug eastwards, forming a single mine gallery that followed the old lane, probing under no-man's-land until a branch split off toward Factory Farm, the former moated farm just to the south of the extreme right-hand end of the impending Allied attack.

In spite of the perceived success of the mines, both in destroying crucial elements of the German front-line positions and garrisons, and in the ghastly effect their detonation had on German morale, there were still some who questioned the effectiveness of the mines. Certainly the 33rd Battalion of the Australian 3rd Division suffered more than most in the Messines campaign. In the diary of the Battalion there is a note from its commanding officer Lieutenant Colonel L.J. Morshead who wrote: 'The crater on our right flank was a

OPPOSITE *Map of the Messines battle front, June 1917, showing front lines and mines.* Ian Passingham

BELOW *A winter view of Ultimo crater looking north towards Messines.*

disadvantage; it restricted the siting of the
new trench, it requires a great deal of labour
and material which could have been more
effectively directed elsewhere, it distinctly
marked our flank and it provided an excellent
target for the enemy. I know of no advantage.'[5]
This was the Factory Farm mine crater, which
had proved a most useful defensive feature for
German Maxim-gun crews who had managed
to infiltrate the position and pin down elements
of the Australian attack. However, had the
farm been left undisturbed they would have
been able to pour fire onto the attackers' flank
unimpeded. At least the initial waves were able
to pass over in relative safety.

Shaking the Pillars of the Earth

Despite the misgivings about the Factory
Farm crater, the mine under the Ultimo trench
certainly did its job. Even today, after almost
a century, it is a visible scar on the landscape.

How much more raw it looked in the aftermath
of the explosion. Yet the destruction seen on
the surface – the huge craters and the infilled
trenches – were only part of the picture. The
mine had been sprung underground; as it
exploded and heaved the earth aloft a massive
shock wave spread through the earth. The
shock wave was part of the way the detonation
of the mines worked: as it travelled through
the ground it collapsed dugouts where the
garrison had taken sanctuary from the barrage
on the surface. Many were simply entombed
and buried alive, others died as the air was
sucked from the shelters, collapsing their lungs
and killing them instantaneously; unknown
numbers of Germans still lie underground on
the battlefield.

Evidence of the massive power of the
mines was demonstrated in Jon's trench to
the north of the Ultimo mine crater, where
the archaeological team found heavy upright
timbers toward the bottom of the trench. As
digging progressed they revealed these as
a timber framework that had thick planks
nailed to them forming walls. Much of the

wood had rotted away but in the lower levels
the waterlogged soil had helped preserve
the timbers. This position is believed to have
been a German trench mortar pit, but what
was clear from the remains is that it had been
destroyed by the mine, not by blast but by
the shock wave in the earth. Investigation of
the structure showed that the timbers on the
southern side of the trench were all leaning
out of the perpendicular, and pushed away
from the source of the blast to the south. The
timber uprights had been battered by the
force of the explosion and left at an angle, still
showing today how effective the mine was.
Due to the waterlogged nature of the ground
and its depth the bottom of the position has
not yet been reached. It may be that the
mortar, its ammunition, or even the crew,
waiting for orders to go into action against the
imminent Allied assault, remain in the ground,
covered by the soils that inundated them as
the earth caved in. However, that remains a
mystery awaiting an answer through further
archaeological excavation.

Gotterdamerung

For the Germans the mine offensive was devastating; 10,000 men are estimated missing from the attacks. Some lie in collapsed dugouts, others remain beneath the ploughsoil; but for others death was swift and their destruction terrible and almost total. As the mines exploded, anyone in their vicinity was torn by the blast and cast aloft along with soil, trench fittings, and all the material and debris of the Front. Fire, hard-edged objects and the abrasive soil of Flanders shredded the men, rendering them down to tiny bone fragments and making the whole area a burial ground. During excavation of Steve's trench just north of the Ultimo crater, the fill of the trench included numerous tiny fragments of bone and scattered personal equipment that were the only traces of the German defenders of the lines before Plugsteert Wood.

These human fragments, spread throughout the fill of the trench, may be compared to the missing of the 11 September 2001 attacks in New York. As the Twin Towers collapsed, those inside were similarly destroyed by the effects of the falling structure on their bodies. At the Front the traces of the Germans became part of the landscape, while in New York the debris was collected and taken to Staten Island, to be sifted and attempts made to identify the missing. No such respect was accorded the Germans, but that is the nature of war. One thing remains the same however: the grief and particularly the uncertainty about the fate of a loved one is identical, whether in New York or a small town in Bavaria.

As has been seen, the effect of the mines was devastating, shattering morale and rendering some defenders so shell-shocked that the initial advance was all but unopposed. Even the debatable attack at Factory Farm had some initial advantages, temporarily knocking out a defensive position for the Germans. However, for the plan to succeed it was essential that the rest of it was followed. That relied on the flesh and blood of the men in the jumping-off trenches waiting for their officers' whistles that would signal the start of the attack.

Following up

The Australian soldiers that assaulted the German lines were able to press their advantage, but there were the twin threats of enfilading fire from Factory Farm and the trenches around it, and from the inevitable German counter-attack. In order to ensure that the ground taken was held, troops had been trained to fortify the crater and turn it into a strongpoint. Because of its position on the higher ground to the north of the lane it was able to dominate the ground to south and south-east, while the raised ground thrown up at the lip of the crater gave good views and fields of fire to the east, toward the German lines being attacked as the assault rolled forward.

Plans in the Australian War Memorial and evidence from aerial photographs all show the saps dug out on the southern, eastern and northern sides of the crater, and on to its summit. These positions were intended to mount Lewis guns in order to pour suppressing fire onto the enemy below and to provide fire support should a counter-attack come from the east. The Australians had practised for exactly this sort of operation on Salisbury Plain: both aerial photos and geophysical surveys have shown T-headed saps extending out from the mine crater that is part of the Bustard Inn trench system. Unfortunately the presence of badgers, a protected species in the UK, has prevented archaeological excavation of this part of the Bustard trenches, which would reveal how the Australians fortified the crater. In Belgium there have been no such problems.

Excavation of the sap facing east revealed a shallow trench, only deep enough to crawl through, and presumably hastily dug, running to a dead end. It had been revetted with a combination of corrugated iron and XPM (expanded metal) and strengthened with wooden revetting frames. Nevertheless, it did not appear to have had a long life as it was never deepened or improved and it became a rubbish dump, where empty tins and bottles, as well as the coke from a brazier were deposited. The southern position was also excavated but this had been significantly altered from its original appearance on the plan. Rather than being a simple affair like the other example, this was a lozenge-shaped position with four deeply dug arms around a central island. This position was 2m deep and had been well constructed with corrugated iron. It appears that this emplacement was deepened and improved while the other was abandoned. This probably reflects the fact that, once altered to its excavated form from the original T-head, the position had fields of fire over a large section of the German front line and rear areas, including ground previously covered by the shallow sap further north. This alteration and abandonment of positions probably also reflect the fact that there was no longer deemed to be a particular threat from the east, following the conclusive defeat of the Germans, while they still held ground to the south and south-east. The emplacement also obviously had regular sentries or gunners posted in it, as one of them appears to have bent over part of the lower sheets of corrugated iron to make a rudimentary seat.

As efforts to consolidate the gains of 7 June 1917 continued, mining came to the fore once more. Soon after the initial successes a Russian sap was blown to create a communication trench across no-man's-land from the Allied trenches to the captured German lines. Russian saps were dug out into no-man's-land as a form of shallow tunnel, so that the enemy could not detect them. They could allow raiders to get close to the enemy, but in this instance it had been dug to allow the transfer of reinforcements and supplies. It was blown, removing the top cover, once the German line had been taken. Meanwhile, the original tunnel used to lay the charges for the two mines was reopened and a staircase dug to the surface somewhere on the north-western face of the Ultimo crater. This work was also intended to allow men and materiel to be brought forward unimpeded by the Germans who still held the ground to the south. This cannot have been easy work in ground thoroughly disturbed by the mine blast and, in its final stages, though the loose soils of the crater lip. Training, it seems, had won the day.

1   Sheldon, 2007: 7–8.
2   Barton, Doyle, and Vandewalle, 2004: 188.
3   Sheldon, 2007: 9.
4   Barton, Doyle, and Vandewalle, 2004: 191.
5   From AWM4 Australian Imperial Force Unit War Diaries, 1914–18 War, Infantry, Item No: 23/50/8, Title: 33rd Infantry Battalion, June 1917.

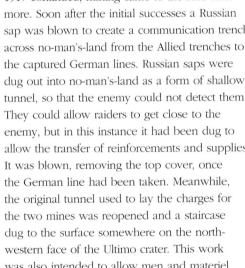

CHAPTER 4

Finding the Front

Before an archaeologist puts a spade in the ground, a huge amount of prior research has been undertaken. Not only have official diary accounts and personal memoirs and letters been read, but much pictorial information has also been gathered. Maps, both those from the pre-war years and trench maps drawn up for intelligence in the war itself, have been scrutinised to establish changes in the landscape and the positions of battle. Aerial photographs too can provide a vast amount of data. This was the first conflict in

which extensive contemporary photographic mapping of the battlefield was accomplished to identify enemy fortifications, obstacles and gun positions, and to factor these into battle plans. From these and the dates given for the photograph, one can observe various nuances of changes in terrain. This can tell the archaeologist where they are likely to gain important data about the conflict zone and those who lived and fought within it.

Once the team arrives on site it is also imperative to gain as much information about

OPPOSITE *Annotated trench map of St Yvon, early 1915.*
Peter Chasseaud

LEFT *Early morning survey work over the German lines at Messines by Peter Masers. These positions are now within the Peace Village.*

the topography of the study area and, through using geophysical survey techniques, to try to establish what lies beneath our feet. Again, this will inform our judgement on where best to target excavation efforts.

The Plugstreet Project was fortunate to list among its numbers, the leading British cartographer of the First World War, Peter Chasseaud. Peter was also the site artist and, as such, spent a large amount of time reading the landscape and establishing an overall context. Peter describes his work in studying the landscape of St Yvon, within our archaeological area.

I did some survey work because I was fascinated by the interrelationship between the landscape of the medieval moated farm (Factory Farm) and the present landscape of water-filled mine crater, earth bank (northern lip) and surrounding trees. I wanted to see whether, without using much in the way of technological aids, I could locate the site of the original moat. Close study of the 1915–17 air photos and trench maps, and comparison with the present ground, convinced me that the old roads, drainage ditches and cultivation boundaries were essentially the same. One ancient ditch in fact formed the southern side of the moat. Other ditches were sited in such a pattern that it was possible, by making visual and graphic prolongations, cuttings, intersections and alignments, to determine the corners and sides of the

moat. In addition, two very old willow trees on the western side of the crater, embedded in the detritus of bricks, earth and concrete, appeared to have regenerated from their original roots or stumps.

Stand by the road, behind Trench 123 where the British front line had been pushed out along the spur into no-man's-land. In the winter there were potatoes or root-crops here. The pea crop has been harvested, and the ground ploughed, harrowed, drilled, rolled – and now neat rows of potato plants are growing fresh green against the yellow-ochre clay soil. There is no sign of the trench and breastwork of the British front line, no discernible depression in the surface. But if you look closely as you walk over the ground (avoiding the crop) you will find green-corroded brass cartridge cases, fragments of rusted barbed wire, whitish-grey lead shrapnel balls, innumerable rusty shell splinters, a clay pipe-stem and bowl. At the field edges you will see rusted shells, exploded and unexploded, empty shrapnel cases, mud-balled grenades, a Stokes mortar bomb, steel corkscrew pickets, and angle-iron ones, for stringing out barbed-wire entanglements.

A hundred and fifty yards away, across the potato field, loom the tall trunks and dark foliage of a wood on the crest and south slope of the spur. This wood was not here before 1914. It has grown, planted, to conceal something else which was not here before 1914 – the German front-line position, known to the British as the Ultimo trench, which was deepened and strengthened between 1914 and 1917, and the mine crater, now water-filled, blown (with its twin at the Ultra trench, Factory Farm, just to the south) on 7 June 1917 at the start of the Battle of Messines.

South of the narrow local road running from St Yvon to Warneton, which is the dividing line between the Ultimo trench to the north and the Ultra trench running through Factory Farm to the south, the landscape is an inversion of that north of the road. While the Ultimo trench north of the road ran up and over the convex

terrain of the St Yvon spur, the Ultra trench
south of the road runs down across soft,
wet cow-poached pasture to the site of the
old moat and ditches, the medieval field
pattern of property boundaries and drains,
of Factory Farm. Here there is also a water-
filled crater, but it lies in the centre of
another, and much more ancient, water-
feature – the rectangular mediaeval moat,
lined on the inside with willow trees, of
Factory Farm. The outline of the old moat,
which shows clearly on the 1914–18 trench
maps (the detail of which was taken from a
19th-century Belgian topographical survey)
and aerial photographs, can still be made

PREVIOUS SPREAD
TOP *No-man's-land
at St Yvon, which was
crossed by the 9th
and 10th Brigades
of the Australian 3rd
Division during their
attack on Messines
Ridge on 7 July 1917.
Note the trench in the
foreground (left).* AWM
E01329P

PREVIOUS SPREAD
BOTTOM *A view of St
Yvon crater. Standing
amidst the debris is
an unidentified soldier
(left), probably a staff
photographer and an
officer (right), possibly
Lieutenant S.H.E.
Young, Commanding
Officer of the
Photographic Section,
Australian War Records
Section.* AWM E05961

OPPOSITE *Map
detail of the area north
east of Plugstreet Wood,
with Factory Farm
centre foreground
and the British and
German trench lines
winding north west
towards La Petite
Douve Farm.* Peter
Chasseaud

*out on the ground, especially after a lot
of heavy rain when the water lies in the
hollows. This is especially notable along the
north side and in the north-west corner
of the moat where the ground turns very
boggy, as I found when making a site-plan
of the moat and laying out the grid for a
contour survey of the surviving northern
lip of the mine crater. The mine was blown,
the charge lying 75ft below ground level,
slightly to the south of the centre of the
moated enclosure, leaving only a narrow
strip of unblown ground, under the
northern lip, between the resultant crater
and the northern side of the moat.*

Contested Ground

Terrain is a crucial element of military
operations; witness the configuration of the
trench lines to the ground-forms and to
significant features such as villages, farms,
isolated houses, woods, roads and ditches. It
is a common misconception that Flanders is
flat. Certainly parts of it are, particularly the
dyked, low-lying 'moeuvres' areas north of
the Houthulst Forest and around Dunkerque
and St Omer. However, there are significant
hill-features, notably the chain of Flanders hills
running west–east: the Mont des Cats, Mont
Rouge, Mont Noir, Kemmelberg, Scherpenberg,
the Messines–Wytschaete Ridge south of Ypres,
the Broodseinde–Passchendaele–Westroosebeke
Ridge to the east of Ypres, and the Pilckem
Ridge to the north-east of that city. The
wetness is emphasised by the watercourses
(rivers, streams – bekes or beeks – and ditches)
and names shown on the map – particularly
the place-name suffixes 'marais' and 'brouck',
both signifying a marsh.

Elevation is crucial for observation in
its various degrees of deliberateness, but
we should remember that this also implies
intervisibility: looking, seeing, watching,
observing, and viewing. Where enemy terrain
was not directly overlooked, the air forces
provided the crucial 'eye in the sky' using
aeroplanes, balloons and kites as observation-
and camera-platforms.

This part of Flanders is generally low
lying, the surface soil being a fine, close-
grained yellow-ochre clay which is notorious
for its impermeability, hence the prevalence
of moated farms. Even on the hills (such
as nearby Hill 63) ponds stay water-filled
throughout the summer, and the mine craters
surviving from the First World War all became
lakes. Any trench or depression (such as a
mine crater or large shell-hole) immediately
fills with water, and so it is necessary to build
up the trenches above ground level with
sandbags and other materials, forming 'high
command' breastworks over 6ft high. This
was done throughout the Ploegsteert Wood
and St Yvon sectors, and indeed practically
everywhere in French and Belgian Flanders
where the geological conditions were similar.
The cold, water-filled trenches of the winter of
1914–15 caused the painful condition of trench
foot, which in bad cases led to gangrene,
amputation and even death. The clay when
wet is particularly cloying, balling on the
boots to form great lumps which can almost
completely impede movement; this has to be
experienced to be understood. In the summer
the clay dries rock-hard, and bullets and shells
would ricochet off the surface.

The 1914–18 aerial photographs of the
Factory Farm area reveal a rural landscape
undergoing transformation under the impact
of war. On the earliest surviving British
(June–July 1915) air photos can be seen the
pattern of roads, woods, farms, drainage
ditches, cultivation boundaries, etc., and
the lush vegetation of the season. The bare
surfaces of roads and tracks, usually meeting at
distinct angles or right-angles, show up white.
Railways form long straights and gentle curves,
punctuated by level crossings and/or bridges.
Knowledge of the direction of light is important
for differentiating between mounds and
hollows; this can be deduced from shadows
thrown by trees, etc. The length of shadows,
related to the time of day and the season of
the year, can give the height of objects. Low
sunlight catches the rims of craters and shell-
holes facing the sun, and casts shadows on
their far side. Long, full shadows reveal hedges
and the types of trees around farms and
along roads and ditches – pollard willows and
poplars. Ground forms and features such as
ditches, breastworks, banks and sunken roads

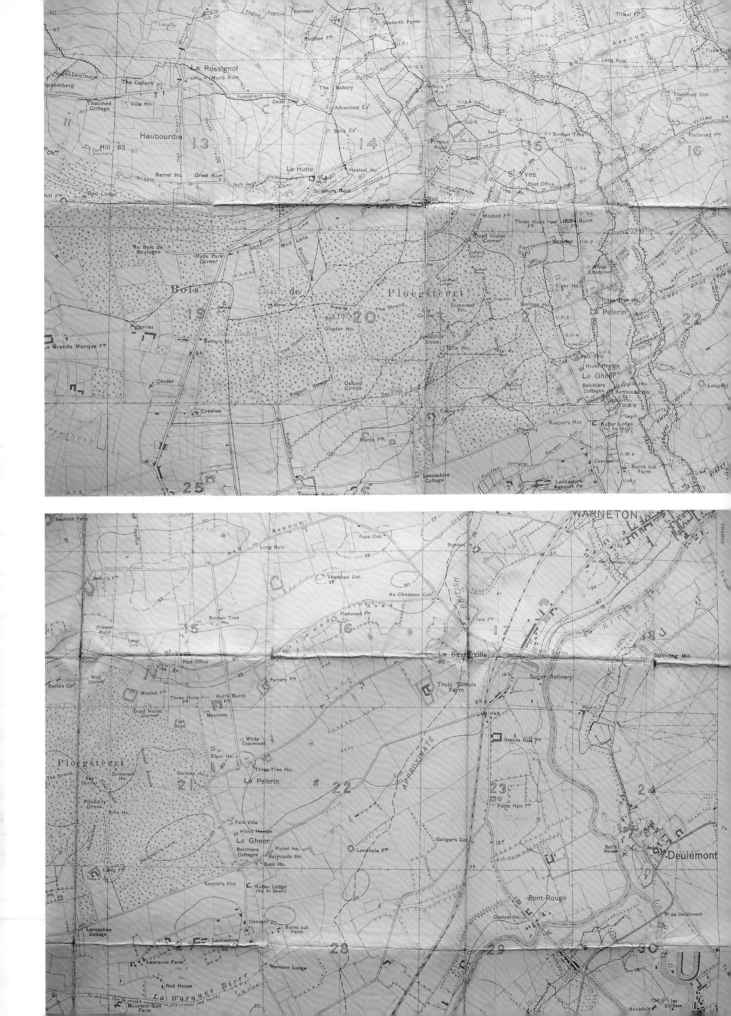

PREVIOUS SPREAD
*Far left: British
reproduction of a
German map of St
Yvon, early 1916; top
right: map of St Yvon
marked 'Secret', May
1917, before the Battle
of Messines; bottom
right: map of St Yvon,
July 1917, after the
battle.* Peter Chasseaud

BELOW *An aerial
view of the early
1916 trench layout at
St Yvon. The British
positions and the
sunken lane are to
the left of the image,
with the German lines
running top left to
bottom centre. Note
the fact that these are
cut into a surviving
pattern of medieval
field systems.* Birger
Stichelbaut

are thrown into sharp relief by the raking early
morning, late afternoon or evening light.

Trenches are clearly shown as zigzagging
dark lines where they are in deep shadow,
while the bare earth or sandbags forming
parapet and parados, reflecting more light,
show up as a pale tone or even as white. Great
breastworks, built up above ground level to
keep the floor of the trench above the water
table, are thrown into relief by raking light
and their massive dimensions made apparent
(6–8ft high, parapet some 20ft thick, parados
less thick). A thin line indicates an elbow rest,
a broader line the firestep, of a fire-trench.
Support and reserve trenches, splinter-proof
dugouts, mortar positions and latrines can also
be made out, though the last three are difficult
to interpret. Machine-gun positions, low in
the German parapet, can be identified by the
thin dark slit of their firing aperture at the
foot of the parapet, by a V-shaped depression
in the parapet, and by their tactically sited
position to obtain the best, usually oblique or
enfilading, field of fire. Typically they were
sited to fire along no-man's-land, particularly
where small salients or re-entrants made
this possible. Where the front lines changed
direction, or formed a distinct bend or 'dog's

leg', the machine guns were again sited to take
advantage of the possibilities of enfilading fire.
Barbed-wire obstacles and entanglements show
as dark bands in front of the fire-trenches.

Farm building and houses are easy to
identify by their shape and context. Roofs catch
the light. If the roofs have disappeared, the
internal wall structure shows them subdivided
into rectangular cells. Moated farms (hence
the German name for Factory Farm: *Wasser
Gut*) show up clearly as a building or cluster
of buildings inside a circular or rectangular
water feature. Depending on the angle of light,
the water in moat, pond or shell-hole can
appear dark or light. After much rain, water-
filled depressions can appear darker than the
surrounding ground. When the snow is on the
ground, the features show up black against
the white ground; much more can be seen on
snow photos, particularly occupied shell-holes,
tracks, blast-marks, and wire.

While dynamic interpretation is much
more fruitful, as it collects data from a series
of images taken at intervals of time, and
draws its conclusions from the changes, or
developments, between each of the series of
images, static interpretation reads the image
as a single text – it draws out what is there,
looking for specific characteristic. In the photo
we can see a medieval and early modern
cultivation system, roads and farm tracks,
and a typical medieval moated farm, overlain
by a relatively simple German trench and
breastwork front system, with communication
trenches running to the rear. The direction of
light and season are given by the shadows of
the trees, which are in full leaf. This photo was
taken in the evening, with the low sunlight
coming from the north-west. The light striking
the front edge of the parapets and paradoses
of trenches and breastworks, and catching the
smooth, reflecting surfaces of bare earth and
sandbags – contrasted with the deep shadows
projected by these features – throws them into
strong relief.

Note the bulging and thickened sections of
breastwork where the Germans have started
building concrete shelters for their front-line
garrison (particularly machine-gun crews) into
and under the parapet. These were at roughly
50m intervals. Machine-gun positions were

sited to fire along no-man's-land, to take an attack in enfilade. They were not generally sited to fire to the front; this would have made their loopholes too conspicuous, and in any case was less effective in terms of a deadly field of fire. Possible trench mortar positions can also be seen behind the German front line. The dark band of barbed wire to the west of the German front breastwork can also be made out. A small sandbag redoubt has been built in the front line where it crosses the road. The fall away of the ground south of the road is indicated by the shadow thrown; the level of Factory Farm is significantly below that of the St Yvon Ridge north of the road. This may explain the old name of Factory Farm – Reebrouck – 'brouck' meaning marsh.

At Factory Farm the German breastworks have been integrated with the ruins of the old farm buildings, giving a typical rectangular pattern. Tree shadows in the farm area show that it has, as yet, been relatively little bombarded, an indicator of the lack of British heavy artillery, mortars and ammunition at this stage of the war. Note how few shell-holes can be seen in the whole area covered by the photograph. Perhaps this reflects the view of this area as being a relatively 'quiet' sector of the Western Front. This would change dramatically in photographic images from spring 1917, when the pock-marked landscape perhaps associated with the First World War has begun to emerge. By the later summer of that year, the traces of battle are all too evident; chief among this are the enormous mine craters and the reconfigured trenches of the new occupying armies.

Not all Those who Wander are Lost – Peter Masters

Although there is a great deal of documentary evidence for the Battle of Messines – for units that fought and for objectives they assaulted – in the 21st century, one can only hope to find partial landscape traces of this sector of the First World War. The two large mine craters of Ultimo and Factory Farm, are still present; some blockhouses can be seen, and there are also some hints of trench-systems which have long been filled in. The rest is hidden; many of the fields here have been under continuous arable cultivation since 1919 and other areas have been planted with trees. Thus, alongside Peter Chasseaud's work in the landscape we needed further methods to assist our investigation.

Fortunately there are techniques available to the archaeologist to make sense of what remains – to see beneath the soil – often without subsequent excavation. Geophysical prospection is extremely useful for detecting buried remains which are no longer visible on the surface or do not appear clearly on aerial photographs. Peter Masters, a leading geophysical surveyor familiar both with forensic and also more traditional

archaeological work, has pioneered landscape-wide surveys in an attempt to read the hidden story of this part of Wallonia.

Two survey techniques were employed with great success at Plugstreet: magnetometry and resistivity. The magnetometer detects the localised magnetic changes in the soil where past human activity has taken place. It is used to determine the presence or absence of sub-surface archaeological features: pits, ditches, kilns, stone walls and even First World War trenches. These sensitive instruments are easily affected by iron, pipes and wire fences as well as any metal carried by the operator. By contrast, resistance survey measures the electrical resistance of the earth's soil moisture content. This is usually achieved with a twin-

BELOW *Peter Masters and Becki Scott use Ground Penetrating Radar equipment to help survey the landscape over the British front line and no-man's-land at St Yvon.*

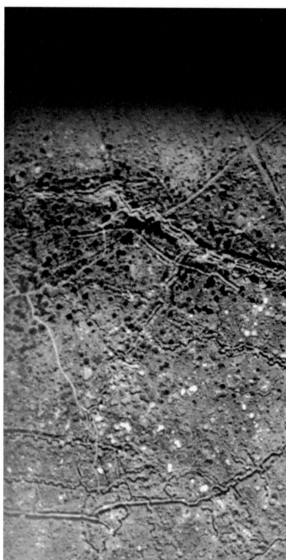

probe configuration – involving a pairing of electrodes, one current and one potential, with one pair remaining in a fixed position (remote probes), and the other (mobile probes) – measuring variations in electrical resistance across the survey grids. Resistivity will identify high resistance anomalies such as walls, metalled tracks and rubble yards or paths, and features with low-resistance values like large pits, ditches, drains and gulleys – normally those which retain water – to a depth of around 1m.

Peter used these techniques at two First World War training areas on Salisbury Plain: Perham Down with its front line, support and reserve as well as communication trenches and redoubts and, of particular note for this study,

the Bustard Inn region. He located the two trench lines along with a mine crater with a T-head sap running from one side of the crater edge. It is remarkable that a clear correlation between this image and an aerial photograph taken by O.G.S. Crawford in the 1920s can be made.

In 2007, a geophysical survey was carried out at Plugstreet across no-man's-land and around the two huge mine craters. Further fieldwork was undertaken in August 2008 until the survey area covered the landscape behind the German front line beyond the Ultimo support line. The survey is truly on a landscape-scale, encompassing some 16 hectares (40 acres). Peter used two pieces of equipment for this research; a Bartington 601-2

BELOW *An aerial photograph taken in 1917 in the aftermath of the Messines attack. Both Ultimo (above) and Factory Farm (lower) craters are now clearly visible.* Birger Stichelbaut

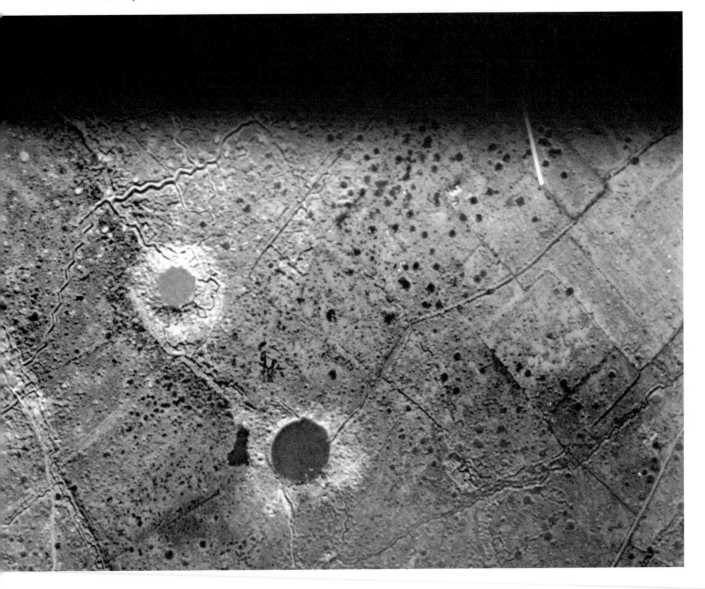

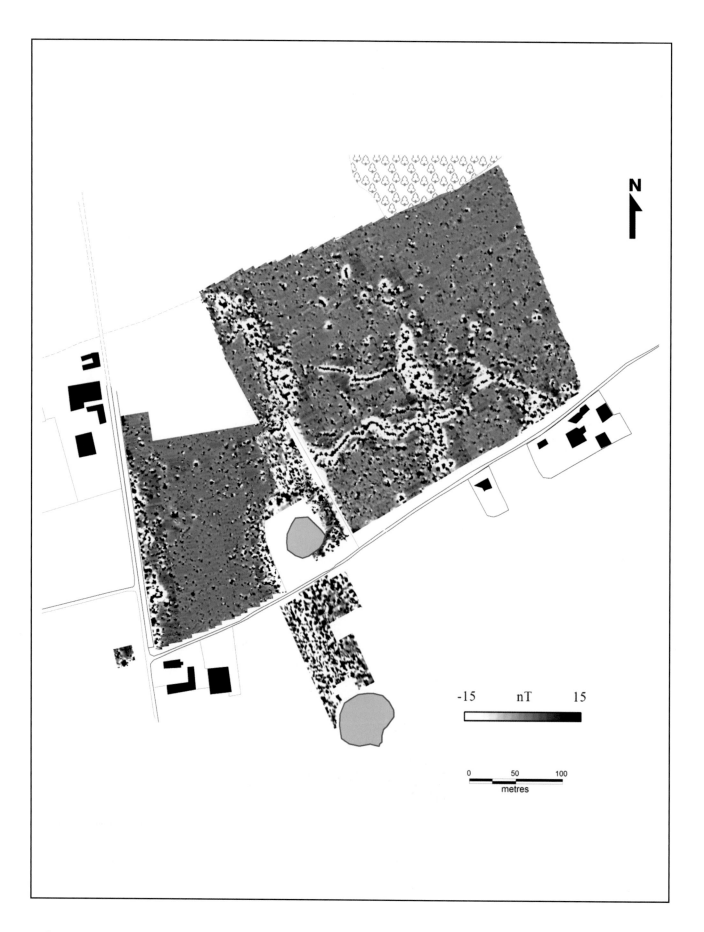

Dual fluxgate gradiometer taking readings at 1m x 0.25m intervals, and a Geoscan Research RM15 resistivity meter with readings taken at 1m intervals and traverse intervals set 1m apart.

The gradiometer results were spectacular, clearly indicating what remains today of the trench lines. The Allied line can be seen running along and parallel to the road to the west of the Ultimo crater. Recently, when the farmer ploughed the ground for his potatoes, he came across what appears to indicate the presence of a concrete blockhouse. This too can be picked out in the survey. Between the British and German lines can be seen a number of surviving shell-holes and a communications trench, which appears on aerial photos taken after the Battle.[1]

The German front line, known by the Allies as the Ultimo trench, was detected, along with its support trench. The Ultimo 'switch' that ran diagonally from behind the Ultimo crater appears as an ephemeral feature. Around the Ultimo crater a number of saps are known to have been dug following the taking of the front line by the Australian Infantry especially for the Lewis-gun positions.

Behind the German line can also be seen where the Australians reconfigured the trenches, including putting in island traverses – not a fortification technique known to have been used by the Germans. Although some shell-craters and a small section of German front line are visible, the survey around the Factory Farm crater did not produce a clear definition of the underlying surviving trench remains due to the upcast from the crater that was levelled across the field by the farmer.

The work of the surveyors had located features that were present in 1914–18 and traced their evolution; the survey had also revealed traces of sub-surface survival and suggested areas that would be informative if investigated further. These endeavours, alongside the work of the historians in the Plugstreet Project team, had provided huge information. It was now the turn of the archaeologists.

[1] Birger Stichelbaut, pers. comm.

OPPOSITE *The geophysical survey of the St Yvon sector of the Messines battlefield by Peter Masters of Cranfield University, and its interpretation. Peter's work has dispelled the myth that there is too much metallic interference on a Great War site for geophysics to work.* Peter Masters

LEFT *Expanded metal (XPM) sheets line the Australian re-cut of the German front line trenches.*

CHAPTER 5

Finding a Better 'Ole

THE ARCHAEOLOGY OF THE ATTACK

In the landscape history of the region, the timescale of the St Yvon area as contested ground was brief. The attacks of June 1917 were an even smaller part of the wider war and yet it was here that the excavation team looked for the archaeological traces of specific events. Could we find elements that illustrated the efficacy of the 3rd Division's training on Salisbury Plain? The archaeological work concentrated around the mine craters at Factory Farm and the Ultimo crater (Trench 122 left and right), the remnants of the German front-line positions, and the Australian attempts to re-fortify them following their capture. These traces, of only a few days of the First World War, nonetheless illustrate the importance of archaeology. St Yvon had been viewed as a comparatively quiet sector, with nothing to hint at the maelstrom that would tear the land asunder in the Messines action. Photographs of the area show relatively little changes to Allied positions up to 1917, while the German positions evolve over time. The pock-marked moonscape of no-man's-land was a thing of other battlefields, with only the occasional trace of artillery barrage visible. This all changed in 1917. The attacks of the Battle of Messines were major components in the story of the war at St Yvon, and thus traces we would find would in many instances be linked back to one specific battle.

OPPOSITE *Belgian bomb disposal expert Gontrand Callewaert holds one of the many pieces of ordnance that still cover the field of Belgium. This is thought to be an improvised demolition charge made from an explosive-filled shell cartridge case.*

LEFT *Sunlight reflects over the water-filled Ultimo crater.*

BELOW *View of
a German pillbox
overturned by the
explosion at the edge of
the southernmost mine
crater opposite St Yvon,
in the Messines sector.
This shelter was one
of many constructed
in the enemy front
line in the Messines
area. The crater was
known as the Ash
Avenue Crater and
was exploded at about
3am on the morning
of 7 June 1917, prior
to the attack by the 9th
Australian Infantry
Brigade on this front,
south of the Douve, in
the Battle of Messines.
Note the thick walls of
the pillbox.* AWM E01269

Gott Mit Uns?
German Positions
at St Yvon

The geophysical survey of the battle front,
along with surface traces of wire, concrete, and
spent munitions, gave an excellent indication
as to where the various positions were located
and, indeed, of what materials they were
constructed, but we were still unsure as to
exactly what we might find. After all, the
accounts of the German trenches encountered
by Allied infantrymen on the morning of
7 June indicate that the mines and artillery
bombardment had done their job to devastating
effect.

Cyril Herborn of the Australian 33rd
Battalion spoke of his recollections of the
German positions at St Yvon in this attack:
'You can't imagine what an awful state we
had his [the German] trenches in, there was
hardly a sign of them and the ground was just
churned up. Barbed wire gave us no trouble, it
was all broken to pieces.'[1]

Written accounts are simply one part of
our understanding of the attack, however.
Australian letters and diaries refer to the lack
of German resistance, bar some fitful artillery
rifle and the machine gun teams at the new
crater at Factory Farm. They note the sheer
devastation of the German positions and yet
fail to mention what survived. One of the
first things the archaeology uncovered was a
bunker, a major concrete blockhouse that was
recorded in neither documents nor maps, yet
was still a substantial structure and certainly
something that would have been an important
strong-point in the German front line as part
of their defences. The later importance of this
feature is covered when we examine the life
of ordinary Belgians living in these fields of
conflict, but there are elements worth noting in
its attributes and role in 1917.

The blockhouse was rectangular in plan
with the entrance facing to the east: the
German support and reserve positions.

ABOVE *Captured German officers under guard outside a recently taken concrete bunker near Langemarck, 12 October 1917.* IWM Q3013

LEFT *The entrance of the German bunker in the front line trenches excavated by No-Man's-Land. The large block is evidence of post-war demolition.*

A dog-legged passageway led to its entrance. The structure had been built through the construction of a skin wall of concrete blocks with iron reinforcement bars (present every 10cm), which had then been strengthened by the addition of a poured concrete face. A number of visitors felt that the blockhouse might have been of an early construction type.[2] The sheer scale of the bunker was impressive: 5.2m from front to back with walls almost 1m thick and a 30cm-thick base, all reinforced with iron bars. Such emplacements were an integral part of German defensive plans, providing interlocking fire for the garrisons, and also enabling a smaller number of troops to shelter from incoming fire and to hold front-line positions as defences increased in strength the further back they went. They were intended to soak up an Allied attack through defence in depth. It was upon these defences that attacks were supposed to founder. However, this purpose would fail when heavy and accurate

ABOVE *Allied trench lines at St Yvon. Note the corrugated iron revetting, remnants of trench boards in the foreground, and the demolished British bunker to the left.*

bombardment by the larger-calibre guns struck home and were followed up by a quick infantry assault. The 33rd Battalion's Official History records that 'Little opposition was met with in the enemy's Front Line. The troops encountered were the 4th and 5th Bavarian Division. The intense barrage had driven most of the garrison to their concrete dug-outs. The rapidity of our assault on the lift of the barrage prevented the enemy from bringing his Machine Guns into action. Only in isolated cases did the enemy show fight and they were easily dealt with.'[3]

Even when withstanding attack, thanks to these fortifications, the life of a German soldier was not an easy one; being within such a strongpoint must have been a terrifying experience. A soldier of the 44th Infantry Regiment of the 2nd (East Prussian) Division at Messines recalled that 'The English have completely smashed in the whole trench and all the dug-outs. I was almost buried in a dug-

out yesterday. It was a concrete one, and the English put a few 38cm shells on it, when it collapsed like a concertina. A whole crowd of men were buried and burnt. . . .'[4]

If this bunker had been fully operational on the morning of 7 June it would have resulted in many casualties among the ranks of the attacking 33rd Battalion, in spite of tactics of bombing clearance laid down by the orders for the battle (with follow-up bayonet work). Indeed, on many occasions little mercy was afforded to occupants of such shelters, which could wreak devastation on the ranks of attackers: '"Kamerad! Kamerad!" And a small bunch of Fritz rush out of the pill-box as we near it. "Kamerad this among yourselves!" And Whang! One of our men has thrown a bomb at them. Terrified, they fly out of the trench. Crack! Crack! Crack! Blaze our rifles and not an enemy is on his feet. They've gone the way most machine-gunners go who leave their surrender too late. War is war.'[5] The very fact

RIGHT *Messines Ridge, Belgium, 11 June 1917. The remains of German Army trenches captured by Allied Forces. Note the wooden hurdle revetment and that its front face still survives.* AWM H15928

that this blockhouse is not mentioned in the Unit diaries, nor in any written records seen by the project team, would tend to suggest that its threat was neutralised in the lead-up to the attack. Given the minutiae of planning that went into the 3rd Division's campaign, it would seem most unlikely that the blockhouse we had seen was not one of those features represented by the terrain model at Petit Pont and is not visible on aerial photographs taken in the run-up to the assault.

Although the blockhouse appears to have been demolished subsequently, there are several photographs of bunkers that were destroyed in the Messines attack around St Yvon, some being rolled like dice by the mine blasts. Many of these images amply illustrate the terror of the barrage suffered by the German defenders, as the detritus of the defeated and their lifeless bodies bear mute, horrific testament. Most of the finds from the area, including German stick grenades, Mauser cases, barbed wire and the metal top of a wicker pannier used to transport German 77mm shells to field guns, hint more at battlefield clearance than the actions of June 1917.

As Cyril Herborn of the 33rd Battalion mentioned, the German trenches had been subjected to a fearful and devastating bombardment. Photographs taken after the battle show the destruction, with the back face of the trenches suffering particularly. Geophysical surveys and trench maps suggested areas that would be worth investigating to reveal the nature of the problem that the Australians encountered when they attempted to 'turn around' German positions. Allied trenches in the area, often lined with corrugated iron, makes the job of distinguishing them in the soil relatively easy for archaeologists, and it also ensures an incredibly strong and clear geophysical signal for the survey team. The revetting of a trench with wicker hurdles in the German fashion is altogether more problematic, given that their organic nature leads to an eventual return to the soil. All the elements of German trench architecture had in some way been altered by Allied forces, presumably those Australian forces that took them in June 1917 and so there were a number

COPYRIGHT IAN.R.CARTWRIGHT 2007

of phases visible in our excavations. The history of the site was encapsulated in small areas of excavation in a way very different to any documentary research.

*Over dozens of broken, smashed trenches.
Dead Fritz are here in their hundreds.
We come to a mine crater. A huge hole
a hundred yards in diameter and thirty
yards deep. The enemy trenches for nearly
a hundred and fifty yards on either
side are blotted out, completely filled in.
Under the explosion they have collapsed,
smothering the men garrisoning them.*[6]

The archaeological team selected an area to excavate on the lip of the Ultimo crater; this was chosen following a close study of survey and mapping results as it was felt that this would prove to be the best opportunity

to study the archaeological traces of the German trench, its destruction, and subsequent re-digging by Allied soldiers, concluding with an episode of post-war filling.

Although it proved difficult to discern the edges of the feature in the early stages, on excavation the destroyed German trench some 3m wide was visible. There was a firestep on the western side, as one would expect, facing the Allied lines. The layers on the eastern side of the trench, including much of the trench furniture one might anticipate – possible sandbag fills and communication cables – indicated that the trench had partially collapsed, presumably from the concussion of the mine detonation, whereupon what remained of the German positions had been filled with debris. Much of this material included large pieces of metal, such as picket-fence posts and girders, which were

subsequently cut away by the Australian infantry on their re-digging of trench positions. This material was probably thrown into the trench as upcast from the explosion of the Ultimo mine.

The face of the German trench looking out over no-man's-land was flecked with pieces of bone and this edge of the trench and the firestep below still held much German infantry equipment: at least two gas mask filter tins, a stick grenade, two ammunition pouches, equipment buckles, and Mauser rounds still in their chargers. Although not a complete human body, there seemed to be strong evidence for the destructive power of the mine in human terms. We found much of the accoutrements of a German infantryman and perhaps even small fragments of a man. This thought was a sobering reminder that when one talks of the 'missing' of the First World War, this does not

necessarily equate with there always being a body somewhere in a foreign field – many simply ceased to exist. Numerous German front-line troops would have been killed by mine blasts, often with little trace of their bodies or equipment surviving. However, taking into account that our excavations concentrated on the destroyed German front-line positions it is perhaps unsurprising that this formed the larger assemblage of military equipment. Given that we excavated the front line trenches that were destroyed at a very early hour of the morning, it must be possible that a large portion of the front-line garrison were sheltered in dug-outs or in blockhouses that were cleared at a later point. There is thus the strong potential that the artefacts recovered in the excavations relate to the sentries that were still on duty at the time of the attack of 7 June. Indeed, the majority of the finds

ABOVE *The small fragment of foot bone found in the forensic trenches by Factory Farm crater.*

RIGHT *A postcard of a German infantry sentry in a trench on the Western Front. Note the gas mask and its tin, ammunition pouches and webbing hooks – all items recovered from our excavations. The* Stahlhelm *dates this picture at 1916 or later.* Ralph Whitehead

were recovered from the sealed elements of the German trench, not truncated by later Australian re-fortification.

During his research, the Plugstreet Project historian, Ralph Whitehead, unearthed a powerful image that was resonant with our discovery. It was a sepia-toned photograph of a German soldier, with the post-1916 panoply of arms, in his gas mask on sentry duty in a sap on the Western Front. His equipment, his location, his duty, all seemed to fit with the artefacts we had recovered; artefacts now twisted and rusted and yet imbued with meaning.

The Australians who arrived at this point shortly after 03:10hr on the morning of the attack cannot have failed to be impressed by the sheer devastation suffered by the Germans and their fortifications. Their orders had been to reverse the German trenches but these trenches no longer existed. The advancing troops had to improvise and so they cut through the remnants of German positions and lined them with corrugated iron, with a certain amount of boarding at the base. The new trenches were around 1.35m (4ft 6in) deep and must have had sandbags added to provide the required height of protection. As one would expect, this area had a quantity of material relating to the attack, in addition to the German infantry equipment found. British rounds in a charger clip and trench wire-cutters were discovered in the Australian re-cut as well as the base of a flare cartridge, perhaps used to send a message to the rear. One can imagine the attacking infantryman being grateful to all these elements as he moved forward, as all would have been integral to a successful attack. If being next to the vast mine crater were not enough, there was much that illustrated the bombardment that the German garrison experienced on this part of the site – burster tubes from shrapnel shells, a live Stokes mortar, the nose cone from a British high-explosive shell (dated 1915 but with a 1917–18 tip adjustment), and many shrapnel balls.

Beyond the area of the mine crater, some 30m to the north and just behind the old German front line, a shallow depression was still visible. The magnetometer signal indicated that this was a feature worth exploring further. Our initial thoughts were that it seemed likely that this was a shell-hole and, as such, was an interesting feature to examine in greater detail. The crater, if that is what it was, was filled with large quantities of material – mainly wire, although bottle glass, some live ammunition and the remains of a German identity disc were found in the material that filled it. The team excavating the feature uncovered a huge depth of soil – far more than could reasonably be explained away as being a shell-hole – until they reached a series of massive timbers. These timber uprights held a number of planks in place, and together they may well be the remnants of a German dugout or a trench mortar position. What was especially impressive about this construction was that, even at a depth of well over a metre, all of the timbers had pushed over in a northerly direction. This was one of the clearest indicators of the power of the shock wave of the mine. A substantial structure, some distance from the centre of the mine had simply been flattened.

Further to the north, the German positions had not collapsed as a result of the mine detonation but had nonetheless suffered greatly in the Messines attack. Although the massive breastwork which protected these fortifications and which formed a large, light, visible smear outside the trenches in aerial photographs was still detectable, the trench had been badly damaged by shellfire with the back face being knocked about. It was this trench that also showed the best evidence for the Australians having turned the line around successfully, just as their orders required them to do. Having removed large quantities of wire, iron girder, and other battlefield material that had been pushed back to fill the trench at some point, the archaeologists found a platform at the back of the German fire-trench. This feature had wooden planks laid upon its surface almost like a laminate floor and represented the new firestep cut into the trench by men of the 3rd Division as they looked out over positions that had once been behind the German lines. This firestep was just one of the elements that infantrymen and pioneers had to construct in order to create a trench line that was defendable, or from which to launch further moves through the positions being vacated by German defenders.

Cyril Herborn of the 33rd Battalion is again worth quoting here: 'After we had reached our objective we had to dig in, put out outposts and sort out the men a bit. . . . We of Co. H.Q.s looked out for a suitable place for our base. This was no later than 3.45am. Then we had to dig hard to make a possie [position], and connect up shell holes for a bit of communication.'[7] When more substantial engineering was required, the Pioneer units undertook major works, yet it should be recalled that these same units had embarked for France with *no* experience of training with duckboards and A-Frames.[8] On reaching the German lines and finding that they had simply been blown away, the whole construction of new lines, especially under fire, must have been a daunting experience, and yet this was successfully achieved. The planning that had taken place in England, France and Belgium meant that all units, including Pioneers, knew what was required of them. The 33rd Battalion History notes the speed at which the construction of levels of cover was achieved in front-line positions, 'Black Line: (a) "D" Company commenced consolidation at 3.30am. And by 7am were down 4 feet 6 inches. By midnight 7–8 June the localities were connected.'[9]

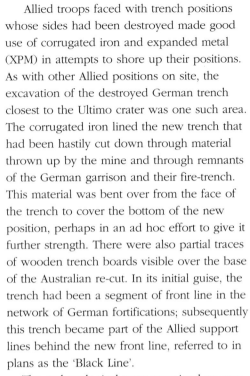

BELOW The view into the German rear lines encountered by attacking Australians, having taken their first objectives on 7 June. This image was taken from the lip of Ultimo crater and shows the commanding field of fire which the Lewis gun teams would have held. Eryka Pownall

Allied troops faced with trench positions whose sides had been destroyed made good use of corrugated iron and expanded metal (XPM) in attempts to shore up their positions. As with other Allied positions on site, the excavation of the destroyed German trench closest to the Ultimo crater was one such area. The corrugated iron lined the new trench that had been hastily cut down through material thrown up by the mine and through remnants of the German garrison and their fire-trench. This material was bent over from the face of the trench to cover the bottom of the new position, perhaps in an ad hoc effort to give it further strength. There were also partial traces of wooden trench boards visible over the base of the Australian re-cut. In its initial guise, the trench had been a segment of front line in the network of German fortifications; subsequently this trench became part of the Allied support lines behind the new front line, referred to in plans as the 'Black Line'.

The archaeological team examined an area which was thought to be a surviving section of German front line known by the Allies as the Ultimo trench – clearly visible as a feature within the modern plantation on site. The results of the geophysical survey seemed, in combination with extant topographic elements, to indicate that this part of the German front line also led to a further concrete-rich depression similar to that revealed as the German blockhouse. On excavation, this feature was in fact seen to be a narrow trench, probably for communication. The sides of the feature were revetted both with expanded metal and also corrugated iron of British pattern. Timber too had been used to shore up the sides, and armoured communications wire was found both at the edge of the feature and also further to the surface. A screw picket, used to hold barbed wire, was found on the eastern side of the cutting and had perhaps once been part of the newly fortified line. The 2m-deep trench was incredibly constricted, with only movement for one person at a time possible, and so perhaps simply reflects a quick attempt to cut through the remains of the German trench which no longer existed as a recognisable feature – the mine having destroyed the former position. The fact that this

seems to lead to a possible blockhouse would tend to suggest that the concrete structure still afforded some protection. Intriguingly, amid the many shrapnel balls, .303 rounds, and an Allied shovel, a 1918-dated fired Mauser round found here illustrated that this once more became contested ground, briefly, in the German spring offensive of 1918 before the Allies crushed German resistance on the Western Front.

This position was almost certainly another example of Australian attempts to re-fortify and 'turn round' the German front-line positions following their advances made in the aftermath of the detonation of the Ultimo mine at 03:10hr on the morning of 7 June. The use of Allied-specific materials (XPM and British-pattern corrugated iron) would only have been possible or indeed desirable in one-event circumstances such as the morning of 7 June. Although the site was contested again in 1918 following its recapture by the Germans in their spring offensives, the Allied forces moved on at a pace whereby occupation of this area was not lengthy enough to warrant major investment in time or materials in trench rebuilding.

A better 'Ole: Australian Positions

"'Look!' And there to the north on the crown of the great black dome we know is Messines hill, we see a movement as of an enormous black tin hat slowly rising out of the hill. Suddenly the great rising mass is shattered into a black cloud of whirling dust as a huge rosette of flame bursts from it and great flames lick, dancing and flickering. High up in the sky above the explosion we see a bank of dark clouds turn red from the reflection of the terrible burst below. A minute or so later, we get the appalling roar, drowning even our guns' firing, as the sound of nineteen great mines going up bursts upon our ears. The ground rumbles, shivers and vibrates under us. The vibration passes on and months of mining and tunnelling work has reached its object, the mines have been fired!'[10]

In diaries, aerial photographs and indeed a visit to the area today, it is the mine craters that dominate. The mines are the footprints of the Battle of Messines. The morale of those Germans who had survived the devastating effects of the blasts, which were audible as far away as London, was crushed but these craters required immediate attention by the attacking Allied forces if they were to gain maximum advantage The decision to detonate the mine at Trench 122, right (Factory Farm) was seen in retrospect to have perhaps been unnecessary and that it had afforded too much cover to German forces, including their machine-gun teams. Remains of trenches here were not visible – it was the remnant of Factory Farm that was of greatest importance, machine-gun parts and incoming Allied rifle bullets notwithstanding. The area around Trench 122, left, the Ultimo crater, was altogether different.

The detonation of the two large mines in this sector by the 3rd Canadian Tunnelling Company meant that the attacking Australians knew they would have much work to carry out to ensure that these newly created positions were fortified and did not fall into the hands of German forces. The importance of this had been emphasised in all aspects of their training from Wiltshire through to the Front.

ABOVE *Destroyed German trenches to the north of Ultimo crater, with Australian re-cut lines with corrugated iron (bottom centre). These trenches had not only been shattered by the mine blast, they had also been filled with large pieces of trench architecture – concrete and metal visible to the left of the excavation section. A great deal of German infantry equipment was recovered from this area as well as fragments of human bone.*

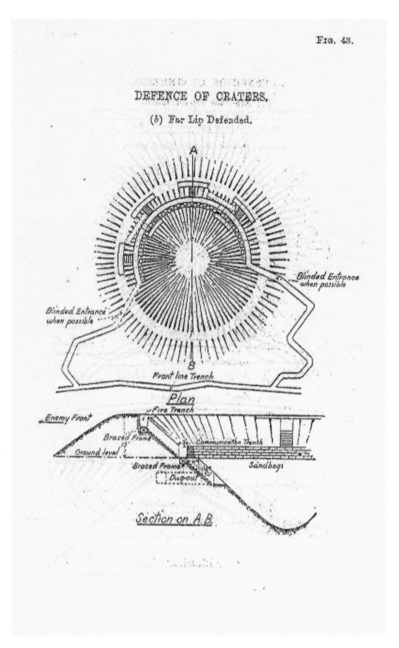

FIG. 43.

DEFENCE OF CRATERS.

(b) Far Lip Defended.

Plan

Section on A.B.

ABOVE *How to fortify mine craters: the 1916 Infantry Field Manual explains the requirement for sandbags, dugouts and firing positions.*

1921 manual, which distilled the experiences of the war and includes diagrams for such defence in Plates 67 and 68), but also the example with which the Battalion had trained at the Bustard on Salisbury Plain. The sketch detailed the requirement for four stations or 'posts' to be cut into the crater lip, all equipped with Lewis guns. The front of the crater facing the Germans was also to be wired with a double apron of barbed wire. As this entity was not cut into German positions but rather into 'fresh' ground, in archaeological terms, associated finds came from an Allied source.

Here we excavated an area where the plan suggested one of the T-head saps for a Lewis-gun position had been located. This had been constructed through the initial digging of a trench whose sides had been revetted with Allied-pattern corrugated iron, laid both vertically and horizontally along the trench wall. This had been further strengthened through metal strips, running vertically down one side, along the trench floor and up the opposite side. This trench might have required such substantial revetment due to the ground being rendered very soft as a result of the mine's actions.

Some of this corrugated iron was now bent over and it covered part of the trench and the remains of a number of sandbags – a situation which would have made movement along the feature impossible. This might relate to an episode of counter-attack shell damage but, as no obvious impact damage was visible and there was dumped material below it, it is perhaps more likely to reflect the deliberate Allied closure of the position. Although elements of boarding were present in the layer filling the feature, none remained in their original positions and it seems as though much of the wooden trench furniture had been removed when the feature went out of use.

Frustratingly, there were no .303 cases in the bottom of this feature which we could analyse to state more positively that we had found the remains of a Lewis-gun position, perhaps one of those that had laid down suppressing fire against the German machine-gun teams once they had infiltrated the lower-lying Factory Farm crater to the south.

This feature displayed two main phases –

This required the digging of new positions into heavily disturbed soil rather than the re-cutting of old trenches and thus was something specific to the battle.

We looked at an area on the lip of the Ultimo crater on its north side following a strong geophysical signal and the location of a plan within the archives of the 33rd Battalion at the Australian War Memorial in Canberra.[11] This plan illustrated the attempts of Allied troops to fortify the crater resulting from the detonation of the mine, and was consistent not only with the practice recommended by the contemporary *Trench Fortification Manual* (the

RIGHT *Antony Roberts and Chantel Summerfield excavate a redoubt placed in the southern edge of Ultimo crater by Allied troops to provide covering fire into the German lines to the south.*

that of construction and immediate use, and a later infilling and decommissioning. If no fired rounds from the machine gun were located, this trench more than made up in material culture reflecting the lives of Allied soldiers in the region, material we shall examine in detail later. This material had been thrown into the position once all salvageable material of use had been taken out. A brazier had been tipped into the trench as a final act of closure. Although this feature had ended its use as a tip, it nonetheless had a power and importance for those who excavated it. Simply to stand in it was to witness the commanding panoramic views it held – certainly enough to give xtensive covering fire to those moving on to the 'Black Line'. It had also been dug, held and perhaps even filled by Australians, men who had fought their first major action and with much of the material we found connected to their lives. For the Australians in our team, this was an experience of kinship, of touching the lives of their countrymen who had fought in a Belgian field some 90 years before; such experiences are something that archaeology affords.

A second sap was excavated on the southern side of the crater but this had been heavily altered in later stages of its use. By contrast to its simple plan shown on the document in the Australian War Memorial the position had been adapted to form a rectangular, four-

LEFT *In excavating the British front line trenches, the team recovered this lump of concrete – the solidified fill of a sandbag. The weave of the bag was still preserved in the concrete.*

FINDING A BETTER 'OLE **93**

sided position, with trenches around an island traverse. This appears to have been done to reinforce the position, which was facing the German trenches to the south, and which remained in enemy hands, even after the Allies had rolled forward to the Black Line to the east. Unlike the other position it had not become a rubbish tip and continued its useful life, watching over the Germans. The expansion of this position increased its fields of fire to east, as well as south and south-east and, as such, rendered the other position redundant.

The position responded to a real threat. In the aftermath of the initial assault the Germans were able to occupy the Factory Farm crater and pour Maxim-gun fire onto the attackers. This swift action, in the face of mines, barrage and assaulting troops, is to be marvelled at but it shows that the Germans remained a potent force. Excavations in this area have previously found human remains of German defenders, while the 2007 work found belted German cartridges from this action. The Australians needed to get guns into position on this flank

of their attack to provide suppressing fire against the Maxim teams harrying them from the south. Once that had been done it was obvious that, as time allowed, the position here would have to be improved to create a redoubt, protecting the Allies' southern flank and preventing German incursions against the strategic position in the crater.

Populating the Battlefield

The spent cartridge cases, the churned earth and the scatters of shrapnel balls all serve as archaeological evidence of the battle. Examination of this materiel allows the archaeologist to develop a picture of the ferocity of the action, of the forces brought to bear on the trenches, wire and concrete. However, as we have seen, materiel and the numerous artefacts also hint at a more human dimension to the battlefield that concerns the archaeologist.

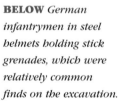

BELOW *German infantrymen in steel helmets holding stick grenades, which were relatively common finds on the excavation.*

By examining the bullets and shell splinters it is possible to divine the nature of the battle, while the adapted trenches bear witness to the dangerous work undertaken by the Pioneers as they struggled to prepare the captured ground for defence against counter-attack. In these ways the archaeology repopulates the landscape, recognising that battles are won and lost by men, rather than coloured blocks on maps or distant, grainy figures on jerky film.

This was particularly thrown into relief by the discovery in 2008 of the body of one of the attackers, lying where he fell in 1917. Although the discovery of a body in 2008 epitomises the human experience of the war, so do the other artefacts recovered elsewhere on the battlefield. Each one has the potential to tell an individual story, whether a sheet of corrugated iron carried across no-man's-land by night by a Pioneer worried that the Germans would open fire, or a pipe stem still bearing the teeth marks of the man who moved to the attack with his pipe clenched in his teeth, perhaps as a gesture of courage and a disguise to his real feelings. Meanwhile, the objects found accompanying the casualty help us see something of an individual person, someone who was more than a soldier but who had a life and personality. In this instance the archaeology of the attack was embodied, literally, rather as it had been in 2007 by the recognition that the spatters of bone in the fill of the German trench by the Ultimo crater were the only surviving traces of the garrison in that area. While the archaeology of attack is the archaeology of mine blast and shellfire, it is essentially an archaeology of individuals who were present and involved, whether as miners, gunners or infantry. Archaeology is, as Mortimer Wheeler said, about 'digging up people'.

Dangerous Artefacts – Rod Scott

The excavators on the Western Front, whatever the age of their site, need to be aware of the presence of unexploded munitions, from the unfired rifle round to the large unexploded shell, which lie beneath the surface. The enormous quantity of munitions around can include high-explosive and chemical weapons, all of which remain hazardous. Indeed, as one of the Explosive Ordnance Disposal (EOD) specialists who works with the team has said; 'It's not like wine, it doesn't improve with age'. Such munitions can still maim and kill and must be factored into the risk assessment of the project. Excavation does not take place without EOD cover.

The Plugstreet Project is fortunate in having serving and retired military personnel, both British and Belgian, with the appropriate training to deal with these objects. When munitions, or suspected munitions, are encountered they are alerted and work on that part of the site ceases. Some finds, such as small-arms ammunitions (SAA), do not require intervention; they are, however, items that require licences to possess, and thus a careful finds policy needs to be planned in advance. Anything of larger calibre, though, is a cause for concern.

Dealing with such objects requires care and knowledge, so the normal team members are sent to a safe distance, allowing the specialist to work unhindered. Where safe to do so, the objects are removed and taken to a specially prepared pit away from the excavation area. In due course the authorities arrive to remove them. If a discovery proves too sensitive for removal there are two options: either work ceases in this area or the object is made safe by in-situ demolition. Fortunately, to date this has not been a necessity on any No Man's Land team site. Everyone is made aware of the procedure. In addition, there is a safety drill for gas, which is practised; so that people know what to do if a chemical weapon is accidentally breached. Visitors to the site often comment on the strips of tape hanging from the trees but they act as indicators of wind direction so that the team know which areas are safe, in the event of an incident. Thankfully this has also not been a problem to date. The identification and ability to deal with chemical munitions is a highly specialised field and, even within the EOD community, one that is only dealt with by specifically trained and equipped personnel.

Prior to the excavation, the directors contact DOVO, the Belgian Army's dedicated service who deal with the 'Iron Harvest', the thousands of shells recovered each year through agriculture, development and archaeological work. They know where and when work will take place and are familiar with the specialists on the team. They will visit at least once during the project and will remove munitions to their base at Houthoulst, where they are made safe. This preparation is vital. As Nick Saunders points out: 'In Belgium, around Ypres, up to 250,000 kilograms of such materials can be recovered in a year – disposed of by the Belgian army on two or three controlled explosions a day.'[12]

Our EOD experts have developed an important working practice for team members when we excavate on sites with live ammunition:

● Plan ahead and have expert advice on hand.
● If you know its ammunition, don't touch it.
● If you don't know what it is – treat it as if it is ammunition.
● Always remember to abide by the laws that govern the possession of ammunition.
● If in doubt – leave the object alone and seek expert assistance.
● Smoking is, of course, banned in or immediately adjacent to excavation trenches!
● Harvesting iron.

The prospect of encountering live ammunition is something that the project team had to consider both on Salisbury Plain and also in Wallonia; the historic accounts told us that there was certainly live artillery fire in Wiltshire as well as the detonation of a mine at the Bustard. Just to the north of the Bustard practice trenches is the current artillery impact area, which has been in existence for a century and has thus led to the current range safety officer for the Plain considering that there are up to 250,000 'blind' (unexploded) rounds still there. These range from mortars right through to huge 1,000lb air-dropped munitions. Our work on the training areas was therefore also subject to close military scrutiny prior to the inception of the project.

Ultimately it seemed as though units that practised throughout the area completed an exemplary post-exercise clean-up with very little by way of ammunition left on site, and all that was encountered having already been fired. The team located the push plate and burster tube of a shrapnel shell but this was the sole element of artillery encountered; .303-calibre Lee Enfield rifle cases were more commonplace, with a number of fired live rounds found in a communications trench. These were dated 1916 and 1917 – the latter indicating use of this practice facility by another unit after the departure of the Australians at the close of 1916. Rather like Roman coins, these artefacts can be very useful in providing dating clues to the use of a feature.

By far the biggest elements of ordnance on the segment of the Western Front we examined were of course the mines. Some 19 of the 21 scheduled to explode in the attacks of 7 June were successfully detonated, one was set off by an electrical storm in 1955 (killing a cow) and one to the south of our region has yet to function. Given the constant reminders of the power of the mine blasts and the effect that 40,000lb of ammonal has, it was a constant relief to look at the two huge craters of Factory Farm and Ultimo and know that the mines in our area had already done their job and no longer posed a risk.

In the planning phase for the excavations, the authors walked over no-man's-land between the British and German lines at St Yvon and we could see that this was to be an area in which we would find much ordnance. As one would expect with a First World War battlefield, the team encountered hundreds of expended, and sometimes live, small-arms cases both Allied and German. These had been manufactured in arsenals from Kynoch and King's Norton in Birmingham to Radway Green in Cheshire, and from Spandau to Dresden and Polte Magdeburg. Although almost all of these rounds were dated to 1916 and before; there were a couple of Mauser cases, intriguingly dated to 1918 and thus resonant of a brief period in the spring of the last year of the war when German forces swept through the British lines in a last, desperate, and ultimately doomed, attempt to defeat the Allies.

Fragments of destruction were also sewn across all areas of the battlefield – shell fuses, some of which displayed evidence for later war

TOP LEFT *The base of a British rifle grenade.*

TOP RIGHT *Fragments of a German stick grenade.*

LEFT *The top of a German stick grenade.*

BOTTOM LEFT *A 3-inch Stokes mortar – still live after 90 years.*

BOTTOM RIGHT *The remnants of a gas grenade. Items like these were used by Australian troops to clear blockhouses and bunkers. All of the team's work was assisted by both Belgian and British ordnance disposal experts.*

adaptation), shell cases, shrapnel balls, push plates, rifle grenade fragments, shell splinters – these are the remnants of jagged, scorching material that killed in thousands. Some of the material had been pushed back into shell-holes, trenches, and craters by those who were faced with clearing the landscape after the war where it lay alongside wire and other scars of battle.

All the above and the revolver or Luger rounds we found were, as stated, relatively easy to deal with and to record, but there were other objects that were more problematic.

Although one viewpoint of an archaeological project would still hold explosives to be an 'artefact' and thus require

on-site recording as to its context and any unusual elements connected with it, once found these objects are removed from site by experts. With the years of war in the region, even one considered to be fairly quiet up until summer 1917, a huge amount of material had been expended. Some of this was relatively new and reflected the changing equipment available to the infantryman. British hand grenades (Mills bombs) and German stick grenades were relatively commonplace and kept our EOD team busy. Grenades come in a multitude of shapes and sizes but most importantly introduce an element of risk in being dealt with. Most grenades have their firing system inbuilt and can function without the requirement for an external weapon being introduced. This means that unless handled by an expert who knows, and more importantly understands, their workings, they pose a potentially lethal hazard to the unwary.

Across the fields examined by the team there were some altogether larger pieces of ordnance: a Vickers 2in mortar, better known as a 'toffee apple', as well as several Newton Stokes mortars; the latter were potentially especially unpleasant as they were at times used to deliver chemical agents. There were also unusual items that were found – a shell case which was now plugged with a wooden bung, found in the region of a feature that may well have been a German trench mortar position. This may have been a demolition charge or an improvised mortar. Either way it was a task for the disposal team.

The archaeological team found shells and shell cases across the site. On First World War battlefields, these come in all forms and sizes, from small 20mm-diameter cannon rounds to 18-inch naval shells. To make shells safe while in storage or transit the fuses were not armed until firing, at which point the extreme forces of the firing process were utilised to remove these safety arrangements and allow the shell to detonate on impact without hazard to the gunners. On any visit to the scene of fighting in the First World War it is immediately clear that not all shells functioned correctly and it was normally the fuse that failed. A conservative estimate on the efficacy of ammunition of the First World War was that

LEFT *This shell case is the remnant of a piece of ordnance that has functioned – note the copper driving band at the base of the case.*

BELOW *Gun crew of a Royal Field Artillery 18pdr battery prepare to open fire near Meteren during the fighting for Hazebrouch, 13 April 1918.* IWM Q8712

ABOVE *The nose cone of a British shell*

BELOW *An Australian howitzer team. Heavy field pieces such as this bombarded the German lines prior to the attack and were successful in neutralising German gun positions, too.*

OPPOSITE *A 9.2in Howitzer of 91st Battery, Royal Garrison Artillery, in position under camouflage netting in readiness for the opening barrage of the Battle of Arras, 1 April 1917.* IWM Q6460

one-third of all shells fired failed to function and were thus 'blinds'.

Shells were given various fillings to achieve different results on the battlefield. These ranged from high explosives to shrapnel (multiple small metal balls not unlike a large shotgun), to pyrotechnic shells that created smokescreens or flares that illuminated the battlefield at night. Of all of these, the munitions which create possibly the greatest problem of all on archaeological sites are those filled with chemical agents. The most common delivery system for chemicals is in a shell and these could range from light artillery, such as the German 77mm, to heavy calibre – the 9.2in Howitzer. Chemical agents either incapacitate, damage, or kill, and by their very design do not require the munition to function to have an effect. The fact that most munitions could at the most basic level

be described as metal containers – and these buried for nearly a hundred years – means that they may no longer be completely intact and the release of the agent, be it in liquid or gaseous form, will be sufficient to affect those coming into contact with it.

Although this material had built up over the years of the war, there were a number of items which were probably directly related to the attacks of 7 June 1917. We found two No 28 grenades, a chemical-filled grenade of a type issued to Australian soldiers to assist in clearing the German dugouts and bunkers during the consolidation phase of the attack, moves which the High Command knew would be a key to success. Although these were not stratified, the likelihood must be that this was the attack in which they were used; they had functioned and yet still retained traces of the chemicals within. The only ammunition that was directly linked to the action was associated with those who died in the fighting. From the German side of the line were the belted machine-gun rounds from the Maxim guns, whose teams died in a brave attempt to retrieve Factory Farm. On the Allied side were the .303 ammunition and Mills bomb carried with the Australian soldier when he fell. The bomb he carried was the one element of his panoply of arms not retained.

1 Edwards, 1996: 42.
2 F. Bostyn, pers. comm.
3 From AWM4, Australian Imperial Force Unit War Diaries, 1914–18 War, Infantry, Item No: 23/50/8, Title: 33rd Infantry Battalion, June 1917).
4 Passingham, 2004: 94.
5 Lynch, 2008: 192, on the Australian infantry clearance of a German blockhouse in the Battle of Messines.
6 Lynch, Ibid.: 187.
7 Edwards, 1996: 42.
8 Molkentin, 2005: 25.
9 From AWM4, Australian Imperial Force Unit War Diaries, 1914–18 War, Infantry, Item No: 23/50/8, Title: 33rd Infantry Battalion, June 1917).
10 Lynch, Ibid.: 183.
11 From AWM4, Australian Imperial Force Unit War Diaries, 1914–18 War, Infantry, Item No: 23/50/8, Title: 33rd Infantry Battalion, June 1917, Appendix 6.
12 Saunders, 2007: 92.

Australian Battery. 9.2 Howitzers

CHAPTER 6

Enduring the Unimaginable

The men at Plugstreet may have been prepared for some aspects of life in the trenches through their training, but not for the experience of their semi-subterranean life. The civilians who had volunteered to serve kings and countries could not imagine what it would actually be like to sit in the earth a matter of yards from an enemy they could not see but who were an eternal presence. Practising 'stand to' at dawn and dusk, when an enemy might emerge from the gloom, was a very different animal from the real thing when the shapes in the mist might be either figments of a strained imagination or a very real threat. Morale and nerve had to be sustained. While training could stand men in good stead, teaching them how to function and stay alive, it was essential that the body also be maintained with regular food but that spirits be kept up, so that the troops remained healthy both physically and mentally.

OPPOSITE *Members of the 45th Battalion in the advanced trenches at Garter Point in the Ypres Sector, 29 September 1917. Identified, foreground, working back: 615 Corporal (Cpl) S.P. Murray; 5330 Private (Pte) Arthur Benfell (killed in action 13 October 1917); 4477 Sergeant C. Smith, DCM; 1669 Pte Charles Archer (killed in action 5 April 1918) (behind Benfell); Lieutenant V. Norton, MC (behind, and to Archer's left); 2015 Pte J.C. Walsh (to Archer's right); 2692 Pte J.D. McLean (to Walsh's left); 4533 Pte T. Eyreington; 3696 Pte Thomas J. Barrow; 2216 Pte Ivens Sattersfield Nobbs; 3458 Pte A.E. Smith (to Nobb's right); 3030 Cpl H. Davis; 4668 Pte L. Davis. The two soldiers in the trenches to left are, left to right: 2240 Pte W.A. Thompson; 2684 Pte H.W. Marr. AWM E00842*

LEFT *Members of the 22nd Battalion, AIF, take a meal in the trenches on Westhoek Ridge on the night before the opening Australian attack on the Third Battle of Ypres, 20 September 1917. Identified, left to right: Mundie, Gilbert, Peach, Robinson, and two unidentified soldiers. Their trench has been reinforced with interwoven twigs. AWM E00739*

Lord Moran's classic psychological text *The Anatomy of Courage* has much to say on the subject of morale, but strangely he omits, or only obliquely refers to, some of the mainstays of morale that are evident in the archaeological record. These include food, drink, tobacco and personal comforts and small expressions of personality in the midst of the ranks.

Marching on their Stomachs

Ask soldiers about their experiences and you probably won't get tales of derring-do but chances are that food will get mentioned, often at some length. Napoleon is supposed to have said that an army marches on its stomach and it seems to be true. If the military experience is, as we are told, 10 per cent terror and 90 per cent boredom, one of the eagerly awaited highlights in the day to alleviates the latter is food, and so much the better if it's hot food. Moran doesn't devote a specific section of his book to food but he does mention the parcels from home that were full of 'edibles' and that even after the loss of friends, meals could become a moment of respite in the horror of war, grounding those left behind through a normal activity.

An inspection of the pocket books carried by British officers and NCOs shows that meals had occupied the mind of the Army prior to the outbreak of war. An extensive supply chain existed to ensure that food was available to soldiers, wherever they were. In the rear areas, field kitchens and bakeries served the men and although food was never going to live up to the variety of menus available to the modern soldier, and largely revolved around stews and pies of meat, potatoes and, in some recipes, vegetables, there were some attempts to enliven the diet with the use of curry powder in some meals, which originated in the Army's service in British India. Today, curry powder is a staple of most larders in Britain but in 1914 it was not a commonplace ingredient. The author's grandmother had curry powder in her cupboard in the late 1960s, probably a link to either her first husband, Gunner George Bowes, a pre-war Regular whose service in the Royal Garrison Artillery had included India, or the author's grandfather who served with the Medical Corps. Curry powder really came into its own when used with salt beef or pork or a product referred to as 'Australian Preserved Meat'. The taste of the preserved meat could at least be partly masked by spices.

When spices were not available men had to rely on more traditional condiments. Excavations on a number of sites in the UK and at the Front have unearthed bottles for brown sauce. This appears to have been such

a staple of trench life that in an Imperial War Museum interview with Private Bert Fearns (2nd/6th Battalion Lancashire Fusiliers) said:

Smells are one of the big things. I can often still smell gas today, and that manly dampness of men and mud at Yeepree comes back when I'm doing the garden. That's all it takes: a sniff and you're back there again. HP sauce does it; hot sweet tea outside on a cold day; misty autumn mornings. Walking past a butcher's brings back 9 October 1917; the blood was in the air after the shrapnel exploded, in the mist.[1]

At the Front the favoured brand seems to have been HP, which still had a description of 'a sauce of high quality' written on the label in French until recently. Meanwhile, the troops at the Cannock Chase camps seem to have enjoyed OK Sauce and an early war midden excavated at Larkhill as part of the Stonehenge Riverside Project, during their investigation of the Neolithic landscape, recovered bottles for 'Ally Sloper's Favourite Relish', which was also a brown sauce that took its name from a pre-war cartoon character from *Ally Sloper's Half Holiday*. Worcestershire Sauce also seems to have been popular and the author has heard of men making rudimentary chutney by mixing it with fruit jam.

Meanwhile, tins for Colman's Mustard have been unearthed on a number of sites. Famously, mundane rations were also supplemented by buying egg and chips from enterprising locals who had stayed close to the combat zone, running estaminets for the troops. Inevitably these establishments, somewhere between pub and greasy spoon café, sought to make healthy profits from the soldiers, as the author's grandfather ruefully commented in his diary on one such: 'They sell nice beer, at a nice price too!' Erskine Williams also wrote home: 'These people make quite a trade out of fried spuds.' Other locally purchased produce intended to enliven the military diet included French mustard, demonstrated by a jar excavated in front-line trenches at St Julien, east of Ypres, where Belgian archaeologists confirmed it was definitely not locally made, suggesting it must

have come from France with a soldier moving between fronts.

If food was monotonous in the battlefield rear areas it could be even worse in the forward trenches. Although efforts were made to transport hot food up to the men in insulated containers, these were not as efficient as modern flasks or the Norwegian containers used by today's British Army: food could arrive tepid or cold after a long journey from the rear. Where possible, it was preferable to eat in the rear lines, away from possible enemy activity – sometimes initiated with the intention to lower morale by disrupting meals – and closer to sources of something warming. This is effectively illustrated by an unpublished German account in the possession of Ralph Whitehead. It describes the situation of 6 June, as the Allied barrage was raging. The author had arrived at the front line, ready to relieve the garrison:

I went to the dugout of the officer in charge to find out if anyone had arrived ahead of me [due to the confusion and difficulties in movement caused by the British guns]. No, nobody was there yet. But as long as I was there he packed up and went back. ... I asked if he wanted something to eat as I knew the food carriers had not got through for the past few nights. He just said, 'Who in Hell wants to eat here?'[2]

At Plugstreet evidence of food was plentiful. The sap dug into the eastern side of the Ultimo crater seems to have quickly become a rubbish dump, including food debris and

a number of bottles. These included a Lyons
cordial bottle, one for HP Sauce, and a bottle
that had contained Eno's Fruit Salts, throwing
light on the diet of the men who occupied
the Messines battlefield. Many books will tell
tales of the diet of soldiers in the line, as do
the many diaries and letters; they speak of
hard-tack biscuits, Bully beef, fruit jam made
by the Tickler Company and of Maconochie's
meat and bean stew. While Army rations were
nutritious enough they often represented a
monotonous round of tinned food. But, it was
these tins that allowed the war to take the form

it did. If troops had been forced to withdraw
to the rear for fresh food the maintenance of
the Front would have been impossible. Indeed,
without industrial methods of processing and
preserving, the feeding of the vast armies
would not have been feasible.

However, much of the tinned food,
especially the Bully beef and the Australian
preserved meat was imported to Britain from
overseas in ships that had to run the U-boat
blockade, making the German tactics of
maritime warfare especially threatening to the
Allies. Despite the constant round of corned
beef in the diet, unusually for First World War
sites occupied by British troops, there have
been no empty corned beef tins found, nor,
thankfully, full tins. In some cases the tin
corrodes but the soil preserves the meat, which
retains a unique odour after 90 years, as one
of the authors can attest from experiences from
another site!

In addition to local purchases, men came
to rely on parcels from home. Fortunately
the postal service was good and foodstuffs,
including cakes, kippers and even faggots –
sent from the West Midlands to men serving
in France – were available to the troops.
Not everyone was fortunate enough to have
a family sending luxuries, so often sections
would pool such things; Erskine Williams tells
as much in a postcard when he thanked his

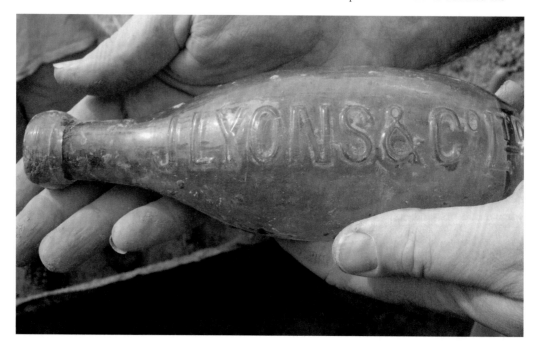

RIGHT *The Lyons
cordial bottle from
the filled-in Lewis gun
position.*

wife for sending a fruit cake, which he and his comrades enjoyed, along with sardines – though he doesn't say if this was at the same time, or as separate courses! Sardines do not appear to have been universally popular though, as one unopened tin had been discarded with the rubbish in the sap. It was found in 2007, unopened, and it has stayed unopened! A bottle of Lyons cordial was also found in the same deposit. Again this was not standard issue and could represent a purchase made during leave or perhaps a gift sent by a mother concerned that her boy wasn't getting the right things to eat and drink.

Today, the modern British soldier enjoys a better standard of food than his great-grandfather but it is still sometimes bland and, if the range of menus is not available, can be monotonous. One soldier who works with the No Man's Land team was looking at the brown sauce bottles and commented that this was why he had never, in 20 years' service, gone on deployment without a bottle of Tabasco Sauce. The quality of the food and its effect on the digestion of the soldiers may also be discerned in the empty bottle of Eno's. This product remains a popular cure for stomach upsets, including bloating and indigestion, something that Bully and hard tack would certainly encourage. The salts did have other uses though, being advertised as a nutritious, health-giving, fruity drink. They

could also be used as a baking powder, as Erskine Childers noted in his pre-war classic *Riddle of the Sands* (1904), while the 1914 *Field Service Pocket Book* includes a recipe for bread using baking powder instead of yeast. This is known in Australia as Damper Bread, which can be cooked on a stick (or bayonet) over a fire. Could it be that the Eno's was carried by someone determined to have hot bread at the Front, or was it the property of the Battalion hypochondriac, along with the cordial bottle and the glass vials that probably contained pills of some kind?

LEFT *A complete tin of fish, probably sardines.*

ABOVE AND BELOW
Lid and complete medicine bottle. Men often bought their own medicines to take into the line.

The capacity of soldiers at the time for personally purchased medicines of this kind is illustrated, for example, by the presence of a branch of Boots the Chemist on Cannock Chase and by similar vials and pill bottles found on other sites, including training trenches near Upavon on Salisbury Plain. In addition to the Eno's bottle, a number of tins have been found that are of the sort used as containers for Andrew's Liver Salts, which could also be utilised as either baking powder or medicine.

Ubiquitous problems of hygiene were also discerned in the discovery of tins that had held either foot or lice powders, reflecting two common concerns of the soldier: the state of his feet – in the face of waterlogged trenches, wet feet and the threat of trench foot, and punishing long marches – as well as the lice infesting his clothes. Both trench foot and lice were of real concern to officers, as they could cause debilitating illness that rendered men unfit for service. As a result, they were expected to check their men's feet regularly for signs of trench foot, while both baths and the fumigation of uniforms was a feature of time spent in the rear area for both sides.

Having food was one thing but how were men to cook it? Far from the cumbersome, horse-drawn field kitchens men had to rely on the arrival of containers, or improvise. The sap excavated also contained the battered remains of a trench brazier and the coke that had been its fuel. The brazier itself was a bucket that had been pierced a number of times on one side; one imagines that the intact side sat against the wall of the trench and was left without holes so heat didn't escape away from the soldiers. The brazier provided warmth but was also a basic cooker on which mess tins could be placed to boil water for tea or for Camp coffee and chicory mix, or where Bully could be cooked to provide a hot meal to raise spirits. Fuel was not always readily available, officially at least, and the semi-demolished state of the sap may represent a search for combustible material

ABOVE *Australian soldiers have their feet inspected for signs of trench foot at Zonnebeke, September 1917.* IWM E (AUS) 1120

BELOW *The stem of a pipe from Australian positions by Ultimo crater. The toothmarks of the owner are still visible.*

LEFT *This was the remnant of the coolant box of a Maxim gun found by Factory Farm crater. It may have been one of those used by the machine gun crew sent to try to retrieve the desperate situation the Germans found themselves in after the detonation of the mines on 7 June 1917.*

either to keep men warm or for cooking purposes. C.P. Blacker commented that:

Trench Braziers were improvised and the demand for fuel grew. The wooden cross pieces of the duckboards and the boarding of the hurdles [revetting the trenches] burned well, and once the discovery was made that these materials could be prised off, they quickly disappeared. Little could be done to stop these depredations. ... It was worse in severe frosts.[3]

It has to be said that fried corned beef and brown sauce remains a taste sensation. Anyone who has spent long periods out in cold weather, something familiar to both soldiers and to most archaeologists, is well aware of the restorative powers of a 'brew' or a bacon roll, or the nearest available equivalent. Indeed, the authentically wet and muddy morning of the exhumation of the missing Anzac in 2008 was made more tolerable by a ready supply of hot, sweet coffee, and for a number of those present, cigarettes. What the excavation team did not get, by contrast to the British soldiers of the First World War, was an issue of rum. Rum came up the line in large ceramic jars stamped SRD (Special Ration Depot) and was used to raise morale and, famously, to stiffen

the resolve prior to attacks or nocturnal forays into no-man's-land.

Interestingly, and by contrast to other sites excavated by the No Man's Land team, rum jars were not in evidence at Plugstreet apart from parts of the British front line excavated in spring 2009. This probably reflects the fact that the Australians did not stay long in the trenches under investigation, as the attack rolled forwards, and that unlike the bottles and tins discarded in the sap the jars were intended for reuse, so rum jars that did arrive here may have been sent back empty to the rear. All other alcohol was forbidden – in case it affected performance – but intriguingly, the German deposits have produced a number of wine bottles and one possible champagne bottle. Can an officer's personal cellar be discerned, or are we seeing evidence of the German practice of sending water up the line in bottles requisitioned from wineries and breweries in the occupied territories?

Whatever the situation with alcohol, water is of paramount importance to men in trenches, away from clean, fresh sources. The British Army used tins, identical to petrol tins, to carry water to the front line, which sometimes got confused, resulting in tainted drinks. No such tins have yet been recovered at Plugstreet, as unusual as the absence of rum jars, but again may reflect their recovery and reuse. It may be that they will turn up in coming seasons – and they should be expected, as the supply of fresh water remains essential to any army.

In addition to food there were other comforts that could keep troops functioning through hardships at the Front. Today tobacco may be frowned upon but during the First World War it was seen as a key component to morale; Queen Mary's Christmas tin, issued to servicemen in 1914 included chocolate and cigarettes, both guaranteed to raise the spirits, and some accounts of the Christmas Truce include details of British and German soldiers swapping their own brands of tobacco, cigars and cigarettes. The rubbish dump on the lip of the Ultimo crater included tins that had contained cigarettes, as well as the Bakelite stem of a pipe.

Meanwhile, a lighter, apparently of good quality manufacture, rather than a Trench Art version made at the Front, was found in the

BELOW *His hands and feet numb with cold, a British sentry keeps watch over no-man's-land.* IWM Q10620

Australian trench cutting through the mine debris filling the German front line. Unless this is evidence of a casualty it was probably a loss keenly felt by the owner next time he had the chance for a cigarette.

The pipe stem had clear impressions of teeth in it, showing perhaps that its owner had bitten down on it during a barrage or had held it tight in his mouth while on the move – the 33rd Battalion History even suggests that men crossed no-man's-land in the opening minutes of the battle with their lit pipes in their mouths: 'smokers even had their pipes out amidst all the fray'. This seems a little exaggerated but perhaps the archaeological evidence suggests not. On the German side tobacco was also an essential of life. To date, fragments of two red ceramic pipes made by manufacturers in Mons have been recovered from the excavations. They were almost certainly purchased while men were on leave in occupied Belgium, perhaps at shops in Warneton, where life continued relatively normally, before the pipes, like their owners, were shattered by the mine blast.

Soothing the Savage Breast

One of the most poignant discoveries of personal kit came from the backfill of the deep German position. The broken parts of a harmonica were recovered from among the other fragments of war. This humble object, like a pipe stem, offers a direct link back to a man and evokes one of the archetypal images of the trenches – men in mud, overlain with a mournful mouth-organ soundtrack. The object signifies a man playing music to express mood, entertain comrades, to raise spirits. Nevertheless, the harmonica could be more than a solitary instrument; on occasion it could also stand in for the military band when men were marching, as the description of men arriving to enlist in the Tyneside Pals' battalions shows: 'one group of about ninety miners ... marching some nine or ten miles into the city, headed by some of their number playing mouth organs'.

This sort of scene would also be replicated during the hunger marches of the 1930s, many of whose participants were war veterans who had come home to find they had not been forging a new world. The quote illustrates the harmonica as a working-class instrument. It was also more portable than a melodeon or mandolin, an important factor for the heavily laden infantryman. Harmonicas, an easily affordable and relatively easy to play instrument, had been popular before the war and the outbreak of hostilities had not diminished their popularity. So favoured were they that Hohner, the largest (and German) manufacturer of these instruments, opened a second factory in Switzerland to meet demand; as a neutral, they could also continue to trade to both allies and enemies. While music may have been a common interest to both sides it was definitely a case of profits *Uber Alles*!

There is no way of knowing whether the harmonica from the excavation belonged to an Australian, Britain or a German and, as such, signifies a common humanity and shared experience that transcends nationality and uniform and which, in turn, represents the tragedy of the First World War.

1 Barton, Doyle, and Vandewalle, 2004: 267.
2 Sheldon, 2007: 27.
3 Holmes, 2004: 319.

ABOVE LEFT *Clay pipe stem from the German lines, stamped 'Mons'.*

ABOVE *The remnants of a harmonica. Both sides played them and the Hohner Company of Germany established a Swiss factory so they could continue to trade with the Allies.*

CHAPTER 7

Across the Wire

In many works on military history and archaeology the enemy is composed of distant figures, sketched in as ciphers to oppose the main subject of the work. At Plugstreet the project has concentrated on trenches dug and occupied by the Germans before the attack in June 1917 which drove them back. The Australians then occupied and modified the captured trenches. The archaeology has revealed much of the Germans who, although absent from the line, are ever-present through their defences and the scattered artefacts, revealed in geophysical survey, aerial photos and the debris of war. In addition, they are ever-present in their casualties, including the men excavated by the Historical Society at Factory Farm. Here Ralph Whitehead, an American member of the No Man's Land team, describes the German troops, who endured mine blasts, barrage and assault by the Anzacs. His research in German divisional histories and the Bavarian archives reveals much about the armies opposing the Allied forces.

Bavaria, Belgium and Pennsylvania – Ralph Whitehead

The German troops facing the Australian attack near Factory Farm in June 1917 belonged to the 4th Bavarian Division from the II Bavarian Army Corps District.

The 4th Division consisted of troops drawn from the districts surrounding Bamberg, Würzburg, Schweinfurt, Metz and Pirmasens. In 1914 the division comprised the 5th, 9th, 5th Reserve and 8th Reserve Bavarian Regiments of infantry. These regiments took part in the opening moves of the war in August 1914 and among other locations fought on the Somme and Flanders in 1914, the Artois, Loos and Hulluch in 1915, including heavy fighting near the Hohenzollern Redoubt in October of that year. During their time in the Artois the regiments took part in extensive mine warfare against the opposing lines, so the men for the most part were no strangers to the devastation of the mine warfare they were to experience in 1917.

OPPOSITE *Some of those who took part in the march to commemorate the 90th anniversary of the Battle of Passchendaele look at results of the excavation.*

BELOW *A German Maxim gun crew of the type sent to hold Factory Farm crater. Note the coolant box to the right of the gun identical to that found on the site in 2007.*
Ralph Whitehead

The division was sent to the Somme in 1916 and was heavily involved in the fighting near Flers-Courcelette. The 9th Bavarian Regiment, in particular the III Battalion (9th, 10th, 11th and 12th Companies), suffered heavily while on the Somme. This battalion had the unfortunate luck of being the regiment facing the first tank attack of the war: the Battle of Flers-Courcelette on 15 September 1916.

The 9th Bavarian Regiment casualties on the Somme

5 officers	182 men killed
20 officers	776 men wounded
20 officers	540 men missing (for the most part killed or taken prisoner)
45 officers	1,498 men (more than half the regimental strength).

After the division was relieved it was sent to a relatively quiet area opposite Ploegsteert Wood where it would remain until mid-June 1917. While in the new position the regiments were able to reorganise the companies and fill up the empty ranks with new recruits. Even though the regiment was at full strength, the numbers of veteran soldiers was considerably less than had been present in 1916 during the heaviest fighting on the Somme.

On 3 June 1917 the 9th Bavarian Infantry Regiment relieved the 5th Bavarian Reserve Regiment due to high losses suffered in heavy enemy shellfire. The position faced Ploegsteert Wood. According to the Bavarians it was not really a wood; the trees were described as 'toothpicks' due to the constant shellfire. The 9th Bavarian Infantry Regiment formed the right wing of the division with the 40th Division to the right and the 5th Bavarian Infantry Regiment to the left. The III Battalion occupied Sector 1A, with the 10th, 12th and 11th Companies in the front line, supported by the 9th Company scattered in small outposts in their rear. The line was considered to be strong; it had been in place since 1914 and many improvements had been made, including a large number of concrete blockhouses and pillboxes.

The men in the 9th Bavarian Infantry Regiment also suffered under the heavy artillery fire. Hot food became impossible to bring up to the front lines. All food and water required carrying parties that took up to 1½ hours of walking over rough terrain just to reach the men. Many of the carriers were killed or wounded in the heavy fire and as a result food and water became scarce at the Front.

According to the regimental records, the night of 6/7 June was particularly quiet. Suddenly at about 4am a series of mine explosions shook the ground like an earthquake and sent huge pillars of fire into the dark sky. The ground appeared to burst apart, trenches and dugouts flew into the air and the greatest part of the III Battalion sector was buried under the debris. Everything became covered in fire, smoke and dust as the enemy artillery saturated the terrain, accompanied by rifle and machine-gun fire. The land to the rear of the III Battalion position where two mines had detonated, Ultimo and Factory Farm, was cut off from the rear by a curtain of impenetrable fire. Almost immediately the Australian troops attacked, using the wall of shell splinters, smoke and dust to mask their advance. The first assaults came in light skirmish waves followed by columns of troops to the rear.

The few dazed survivors of the German 12th Company, the right wing of the 11th Company, and left wing of the 10th Company, were soon overwhelmed in the attack that quickly occupied the German positions and outflanked the neighbouring units. The supporting 9th Company was suddenly faced with a massive assault and those not killed were for the most part wounded or captured. The two companies assigned to the division boundary attempted to counter-attack but were swiftly surrounded by Australian troops. and most ended up as POWs.

The men occupying the rear positions in the second line could not advance through the wall of fire, and held on to their positions despite the heavy fire directed against them. The second positions also resisted the enemy pressure and soon became the new front line.

The neighbouring 1st Company 5th Bavarian Infantry Regiment holding the line near the Factory Farm crater reacted quickly to the attack. While the company was forced to curve their line back to the rear in order to prevent it from becoming outflanked, fresh reserves were rapidly assembled and moved forward to prevent any chance of an enemy breakthrough in their direction. *Leutnant der Reserve* Eck, Commanding 2nd Company, hastily brought up three machine guns into position in and around the newly formed Factory Farm crater and effectively flanked the enemy advance. The men excavated in this area were probably part of this action. In addition, a 7.92 round, still retaining part of the fabric belt that would have fed it through the Maxim gun was uncovered. The date on the bottom of the cartridge was 1917, suggesting that it came from the ammunition taken into the crater by Eck's men and lost after the firefight with the Anzacs, during which the German troops found nearby were probably killed.

Later in the evening the new lines were consolidated and reinforced in order to maintain the stability of the Front.

The 9th Bavarian Infantry Regiment losses in the Australian attack

7 officers	75 men killed
9 officers	442 men wounded
10 officers	353 men missing (majority killed in the mine explosions or captured)
26 officers	870 men (wounded or killed).

Once again the 12th Company suffered the most losses including 2 officers and 53 men killed. Overall, the III battalion lost 5 officers and 173 men killed in the attack. Of these only 45 have known burials, all in the mass grave located at the German cemetery in Langemark.

Of the men who have no known resting place one in particular has a unique meaning to the author: *Infanterist* Heinrich Schmitt, 12th Company, 9th Bavarian Infantry Regiment, who was born on 27 August 1892 in New York, 'Nord Amerika'. In researching possible matches it is believed he was born in Queens County, New York as Henry Schmitt. Heinrich (or Henry) was one of six men in the 9th Bavarian Infantry Regiment who were born in Pennsylvania or New York to die in the ranks of this regiment. Undoubtedly there were more who served and survived the war. Their presence opens up an entirely new area of research into the history of this period and demonstrates the truly global nature of the war.

Excavating the Enemy

Archaeological traces of the Germans are, of course, found across the study area. They include elements of uniform and the leather webbing worn by the soldiers. In the area of trench excavated close to the Ultimo crater the material recovered included filters from gas masks, fragments from ammunition pouches

LEFT *The filter tin of a German respirator – one of two found with German infantry equipment in the destroyed German front lines by Ultimo crater.*

and fastenings from webbing, as well as heads from grenades. All of these are the personal, issued kit from soldiers. They were recovered from the fill of the trench that was deposited there by the mine blast. The upcast included trench furniture, materiel and the garrison that had been blown skywards. The tiny fragments of bone scattered among the debris probably represented the soldiers but the presence of an amount of equipment also suggested that these were men and that the only tangible traces were the durable elements of their kit, as soft tissue and bone had been ground to dust by explosion and the abrasive qualities of the soil. At Langemarck the thousands of names recorded in the German cemetery are the only memorial to these vanished men, save for the archaeological objects that mark their passing.

DEINZER M...
MICHAEL INFANTER...
WILHELM RESERVIST †22.8...
TIER †6.8.1914 · DELHÄS PETER M...
LIUS KURT FAHNENJUNKER †6.8.1914
Z GEFREITER †4.10.1917 · DELLING MAX SCHU...
VIST · DEMANT AUGUST KANONIER †29.10.1918
DEMMELMAIER JOSEPH INFANTERIST †7.6.1917
DENGLER GEORG ERSATZ-RESERVIST †24.5.1915
†16.6.1915 · DENGLER JAKOB GEFREITER †16.6.1915
7 · DENGLER WILHELM ERSATZ-RESERVIST †16.6.19 15
POLD JÄGER †4.5.1918 · DENNER ADOLF GEFREITER †2
IER †4.11.1914 · DENNERT HANS GEFREITER † 6.8.191
1918 · DENZINGER HEINRICH WEHRMANN † 13.11.1914
14 · DEPPE HERMANN RESERVIST †22.8.1914 · DEPPE
RONARD UNTEROFFIZIER †22.8.1914 · DEPPISCH JAKO
EROFFIZIER †10.11.1914 · DERLE LOUIS SERGEANT †3.11.19
1918 · DERSCH HEINRICH GEFREITER † 11.11.1914
DARALD LANDSTURMMANN †28.10.1917 · DESMAROWITZ
JÄGER †5.11.1918 · DETTELBACHER EUGEN MUSKETIER
DEINZER HERMANN DETTLOFF ARTHUR IZEFELDWEBEL
N UNTEROFFIZIER †22.8.1914 · DEUS ERNST MUSKETIER KONRAD
MANN †10.11.1914 · DEUTSCHER LANDSTURM
45.1918 · DEUTSCHER LANDSTURM †2.12.1917
45.1918 · DEUTSCHER LANDSTURM
DENTSCH DICKE

ABOVE *'The Silver Bullet', a game in which players rolled balls through trenches to reach Berlin. This example was given to Belgian children by British troops and has become a family heirloom.*

The Absent Victims

One afternoon in summer 2008, a local man with two small children in tow approached one of the excavation trenches at St Yvon carrying an object that he wanted to show to the archaeologists; something 'unique: you won't find this anywhere else'. The object was a small board game entitled 'The Silver Bullet or the Road to Berlin', given to his grandmother by a British soldier in 1916 on the eve of her departure for Normandy, where she and her family were to be refugees until the end of the war. 'She saw the soldiers playing with it every night and they taught her how to play it, so when she left one of them gave it to her as a parting gift'. Much later on, back in the Ploegsteert area, 'my father played with it and later I played with it – my children still play with it today'.

This unusual object and the story relating to it allude to a relatively little known aspect of the First World War on the Western Front: the experience of civilians who found themselves in the areas of combat. This experience included foreign occupation for those caught behind German lines,[1] and evacuation,[2] and the damage or destruction of countryside and buildings, loss of property and sometimes of life on both sides of the front line.[3] These experiences and the phase of reconstruction have not been greatly memorialised or recorded and today few survivors are still alive to tell the story but, as with our visitors' game, some traces remain allowing us to reconstruct that experience: both historical traces and received memories among the local population of the former battlefields.

Meanwhile, the story of civilian involvement is also told by the archaeological remains in the area. Perhaps the two most noticeable reminders of the war at St Yvon are the two water-filled mine craters, reminders of the awesome power of the explosives detonated beneath the Germans in June 1917. The Factory Farm crater was blown beneath a moated farm that had been occupied and then defended by the Germans in 1914. Throughout the period from late 1914 to June 1917 they had reinforced the position, creating a strongpoint that dominated the land to both front and south, but also gave a view across the lane toward the British Trench 122. Any attack from here toward the German positions to the north would be skylined as the land rises. Machine guns could enfilade the attackers and cause maximum casualties. Unfortunately, the higher ground to the north had to be taken and it was not an option. The Australian 3rd Division would be attacking across this very ground and so Factory Farm had to be neutralised. An assault on the farm would have to cross boggy ground and be exposed to German fire, not only from the farm but also the trenches to the south. Artillery might knock out the garrison; a mine certainly would.

The blast that ensued destroyed all trace of the moat, the farm that had been sited on it since medieval times, the defences, and all the German soldiers occupying it. In a single devastating moment it was all gone, but since it was the last mine to be blown the garrison must have seen the pillars of fire advancing swiftly toward them and shaking their world as the Ultimo mine was detonated. Their last thoughts must have been where it would end. Unluckily for them it was beneath their feet.

Factory Farm was an obvious target for the archaeological excavation. There were several reasons for doing this: not only did upcast from the mine crater include material from the German defences – which would give an indication of how strong they were and how they had been constructed – but also the landowner had removed part of it in an attempt to raise the level of the rest of the field to make a drier pasture for his cattle. In doing so he had discovered two German skeletons which were subsequently recovered by members of the local Historical Society. The Society asked the team to record such of the crater lip as still survived so that it was at least preserved by record. Two trenches were cut into the upcast earth and a third was opened where the bodies were found, as there had been some debate about whether all the remains had been excavated.

Excavations close to a twisted metal beam were intended to reveal details of the fortifications. Unfortunately all that this area revealed were the mixed soils of the crater lip, thrown up by the blast. However, the other section that cut into the mounded soils was much more revealing, indicating far more about the story of the site than the team had imagined. Rather than exposing traces of the German defences the excavators found a large section of brick wall. The age of the brick and the lime mortar used in their bonding showed that this was not a German defence but a relic of the pre-war farm. Interestingly, despite other evidence of the power and heat of the mine blast this chunk of brickwork, about 1m x 1½m in size, had not been blown to bits, and nearby finds had also survived reasonably well, showing that a blast is a complex event, destroying some things and leaving others. As excavation continued a number of illuminating objects not atomised by the mine were recovered. These included horse harness, domestic pottery, textiles, and a domestic stone mortar that was at least 300 years old, an antique even by the outbreak of war.

The mortar was typical of the type found across western Europe in the later- and post-

ABOVE *Two of the excavation team, Ralph Whitehead and Birger Stichelbaut, during a rare moment of rest in the excavations of German lines in 2007.*

LEFT *The stone mortar (mixing bowl) found amongst the destroyed remnants of Factory Farm. Note the soil on the interior, garden soil which still adhered to the object.*

medieval periods. They were the food processors of their age, used for the grinding of herbs and spices and for the mixing of sauces, marinades and other mixtures for the kitchen. This one had been carved from stone, with a pouring lip and lugs for ease of lifting. By 1914 such objects had fallen out of use as lighter, cheaper ceramic alternatives became available and cooking styles changed. However, the mortar had not simply been discarded; on excavation it was found to have traces of light garden soils inside it that contrasted markedly with the heavy soils surrounding the farm, suggesting that it had enjoyed a second role as a planter for flowers. This one item gave an insight into the quiet domesticity of civilian life, with flowers beautifying the homestead. The planter probably continued to add a splash of colour to the site once the German garrison arrived in 1914 – it is not impossible that one of the occupiers continued their interest in cultivation as a moment of humanity in the midst of the conflict.

The horse harness was of civilian type, which was no surprise, as the occupied farm was too close to the British trenches for horses to have been brought up by the Germans. It lay in a heap at the bottom of the excavation trench. Horses were fundamental to farming in the years before 1914. They were used for draught work, pulling farm machinery and carts, doing the jobs now taken by tractors and combines. As such, the excavated tangle of leather and brass offered an insight into the daily toil of the farm and its social structure, since horses required specialists to work them, such as ploughboys and carters, who may have lived on the site. In addition, the objects

tied the farm into a wider network, including farriers, wainwrights and saddlers, who shod the animals and provided the vehicles and tack to enable the farmer to work his land.

Other artefacts offered further understanding of the domestic life of the farm. Pottery and china illustrated the kitchen and table wares used by the family and their labourers, and a crystal wine glass indicated not only consumption of wines but also the social standing or aspirations of the family. It may be that the fine wine glasses and fine china only came out of the cupboard for festivities and funerals but it was there, either on display in the china cabinet or in use on the table. Visitors to this part of Europe will know the importance of family gatherings, centred on the table, and these fragmentary objects offer a glimpse of life at the farm in the years before the arrival of the foreign armies. However, the power of the mine was also demonstrated by these objects for a piece of china saucer had a piece of glass melted to it – which indicates temperatures in excess of 1,000 degrees Celsius needed to liquefy it – while fragments of vitrified ceramics were recovered nearby. Meanwhile, a quantity of finely woven fabric was also recovered from the same context. It was too fine to be either some remnant of the German Army's presence, or curtains left up at the windows when the family departed. Examination suggested that the cloth was made of silk. It had been dyed black by the soil and no woven pattern was seen but it has been suggested that this may have been the remains of a dress abandoned by the family.

All of these domestic and agricultural objects, as well as the shattered wall, demonstrated something fundamentally important and frequently forgotten in conflict archaeology – that the landscape is not a blank canvas onto which soldiers march, fight and die. rather it is, in most cases, a domesticated landscape where civilians live and work; where they have their homes and from which they may be forced to flee.

In wars before 1914 armies had swept through this region, looting, fighting and occupying towns but the First World War was different for the civilians as much as for the combatants. This was not a war where the armies would pass on and life could resume, after a fashion. Instead, the fossilisation of the Front and the deep reserve

ABOVE *The excavation team examine the crater lip at Factory Farm. This site was heavily fought over on 7 June as German machine gun teams looked to make use of the cover created by the crater.*

areas of defences, camps, gun lines, depots and all the infrastructure necessary to support the armies would occupy large areas of ground. Whole tracts of land were militarised into a wider battlescape beyond the battlefield in this new era of total war.

As entire landscapes were taken into military control, civilians were forced from their homes. While some families moved short distances to the rear and tried to make money selling souvenirs, food, drink and services to the soldiers on their way up the line, many others fled. The area of Ploegsteert was a battlefield throughout the war, and locals experienced evacuation and extreme damage to both built and rural landscape.[4] Civilians began to leave Ploegsteert during 1914 and 1915 and few remained by 1916, when a German offensive and bombardments destroying a large number of houses led to a formal order of evacuation by the British military authorities.[5] The refugees journeyed towards the interior of France, some as far as Normandy or the Ardèche, but others to nearby Haezebrouck or even Nieppe, a few miles south-west of Ploegsteert (though this village, too, had to be evacuated during the last German offensive in April 1918).[6] Such reluctance to leave was common all along the Western Front[7] and may explain why some Ploegsteert residents applied to return to the area even before the armistice, in October to early November 1918.

Some refugees made their way to Britain (one fictional refugee was Agatha Christie's Poirot). Meanwhile, others fled overseas to the Americas to get as far from the war as possible. One such group was aided by a member of their community who had already emigrated to the United States and who returned to assist his fellow countrymen displaced by the fighting.[8] The artefacts recovered from the lip of the Factory Farm crater embody a civilian experience of trauma and dislocation to life that would continue for many years Like the recruits of 1914, these civilians probably also expected the war to be 'over before Christmas', when they would, as their ancestors had, return to the land, rebuild and carry on. But it was not to be. The fine china, wine glasses and dresses were abandoned as the family took to their heels in the face of the German onslaught and the arrival of the British forces to oppose them. These articles remained in the house for the Germans to discover when they arrived as the occupiers, and it may be that the family's best tableware found itself being used for the meals of the invaders. For a farming community, becoming refugees was more than a displacement, it was a total loss of livelihood. These were people who were tied to land that had now become a battlefield; it was their source of income but more than that it was home in a very deep sense because they were part of the landscape from which they had been forced.

[1] See eg Cobb, 1983; McFail, 2001, and Van der Meersch, 1930, for a fictional account.
[2] See eg Nivet, 2004.
[3] See eg Clout, 1996; Recontructions, 2000; Duménil and Nivet, 2003, for France; Walle, 1978; Bourgeois, 1978; Parez, 1978; Carnel, 2002, for the Ploegsteert area.
[4] See Walle, 1978; see also Bourgeois, 1978, and Parez, 1978, for Comines-Warneton; and Carnel, 2002, for Neuve-Eglise.
[5] Walle, Ibid.: 473, 461.
[6] Walle, Ibid.: 462.
[7] See eg Clout, Ibid.: 60 ff.
[8] Marylane Barfield, pers. comm.

CHAPTER 8

The Return of the Native

While the fear of flight might diminish with time and optimism about a homecoming grow with the news of German retreat, nothing was going to prepare the refugees for the situation they would find on their return. Images of the devastation wrought on the land of the Front by prolonged artillery barrage are well known. The returning Belgians found an indescribable and unrecognisable landscape covered by networks of trenches, netted by thickets of barbed wire, tunnelled by dugouts, battered by shells that had destroyed all traces of habitation and almost every stick of woodland, and scattered with cemeteries that had been created by all nations on once-prime farmland. In the low-lying ground of Flanders, drainage ditches were broken and land flooded, trenches had been breastworked, standing proud above the wet ground, and both sides had built reinforced concrete bunkers, as part of their defence systems.

Yet those scenes depicted by photographs and Nash paintings of the scorched landscapes of the Western Front, do not convey the full horror awaiting the natives. Whole areas were poisoned by gas residues – including pools of mustard gas that still waited to burn the unwary – and thousands of unexploded shells and grenades littered the land to such an extent that even today farmers and builders still turn up tons of munitions each year, and accidental deaths are an annual occurrence.

Meanwhile, the thousands of missing men lay in the battered earth, not the clean skeletons that are unearthed today but corrupt cadavers wearing tattered uniforms and still bearing arms in death. Some settlements were recognisable only by a bend in the river or concentrations of rubble around what was once the town square but for some unfortunates everything had gone. Following the Battle of Messines, 2nd Lieutenant Arthur Cooper of the Australian 33rd Battalion was moved to comment: 'Poor old Europe, her buildings and churches have been knocked about lamentably. It will take years of re-construction to bring her back to a state anything like which existed before the war.'[1]

On return the locals found a 'desolate and macabre spectacle' of ruins, shell-holes and corpses or, in another account, 'a desert with birds of prey flying overhead'[2] Some returnees immediately built makeshift shelters on the sites of their former property, using the materials and ruins lying around; others occupied concrete bunkers, and yet others from 1919 received former military huts from the British Army working locally to clear and recover materials and to dispose of the ordnance.

Initially, living conditions were grim: the temporary dwellings were cold and damp and invaded by rats, and bread and other provisions only gradually became available and for a time had to be procured at considerable distance. Eventually better-quality temporary housing was provided by the Belgian government that from 1919 sent prefabricated

ABOVE *An image of devastation: all that remained of Delville Wood on the Somme after months of shelling. At Plugstreet and Messines, the returning Belgians found an indescribable and unrecognisable landscape that once was their home.* IWM Q4417

wooden housing with concrete foundations. Gradually a few shops returned to Ploegsteert, including a baker and a general store/café; and the local council, school and chapel were established in temporary huts. An agricultural union was created to assist farmers in procuring cattle and other farming provisions. A few villagers found work in nearby France but many others needed financial assistance, provided by the Belgian state from mid-1920.

Clearance and ordnance disposal continued by teams of Chinese workers under orders of the British Army, known locally as 'Annamites', accommodated in temporary camps on the former battlefield, including one at Mont de la Hutte and one at le Gheer.[3] Rebuilding began in earnest in 1920, sponsored by the Belgian Office des Régions Dévastées that issued subsidies and materials to private individuals for building semi-definitive housing. However,

roads were not properly resurfaced until 1923, by which time only around two-thirds of the pre-war population had returned to Ploegsteert and around half in the area as a whole.

Many did not return at all, and this is still clearly remembered by today's inhabitants, as interviews with local people conducted in tandem with the excavations have revealed. It is said that the elders were reluctant to speak about the wartime: 'they saw too much, they lived too much'. But many today can still relate details of that period, often intermingled with personal or received memories from the Second World War when the area was once again occupied by Germans with a theatre of (more limited) combat.

Many refugees did not return because they found jobs and often a spouse where they had gone, and were welcomed by the French who knew that they were not parasites and were

PLOEGSTEERT – MESSINES ROAD

ESSEX. FARM.

hard working. Even the Flamands, who didn't speak French, were welcomed with open arms. Some took over large farms which no longer had a farmer. Many returned, such as young farmers back from the war, only to leave again to find work on farms in France (often presumably filling up places opened up by war losses).[4] 'They went to farms, they worked hard: it's the Flamand mentality,' said a man of his great-uncles, all former soldiers, who in 1922 left again for farms in Normandy. This man's grandfather on the other hand had been exempted from military service and stayed put throughout the war, when his farm had acted as the British HQ (and famously hosted Churchill): 'He stayed because someone had to look after the animals.'

The fact that many had to leave to find work after the war is partly explained by the fact that wealthy owners of factories, land or other businesses, many of them French, did not return because they were not entitled to war reparations and could not afford to reconstruct, or because they were in a hurry to restart their business and did not want to

wait for reconstruction. Those who left in the immediate post-war years are also said to have been forced away by hardship: the area had already been poor before the war, and farmers had been mostly tenants who had 'only owned tiny plots and a few small animals'. The war meant that 'they had nothing, there was nothing left' - or, as an elderly informant put it graphically, alluding to the utter devastation of the land: 'all they had left was holes'.

Nevertheless, many returned and stayed, and undertook the hard and thankless task of re-creating a habitable place to live. Typical comments of those times included: 'When my parents returned after being refugees, they filled up all the shell-holes with shells, barbed wire and so on. They put it all in and covered it up with earth – all of it by hand', and 'When my mother and her family returned from France, they built a temporary wooden house

ABOVE *The photographs of Plugstreet and Messines after the battle that appear above and on pages 126, 128 and 129, are courtesy of the Messines Historical Society.* Jean-Michel Van Elslande

[baraque] by the river, and every day they walked two kilometres to the farm to level the land, to fill in the holes.' According to one account, some locals profited from this process of clearance and restoration: one entrepreneur is said to have charged '5 francs for filling a small hole and 10 francs for a large hole – a lot of money at that time. There were teams doing the clearance; they came and counted the holes: so many holes, so much money charged'. A different view was that of children: 'My grandmother was a child [then] and she remembered how she loved living and going to school and to Church in the temporary buildings, and the freedom of going around when there were no cars, no roads, nothing.'

A narrative about one particular reconstruction was given by interviewees, the present-day owners of a farm reconstructed at St Yvon following the destruction of the pre-existing buildings through the Factory Farm mine blast. They recall that before the war the farm had been owned by a family of French industrialists, who rented it to a farmer who left the area at the war's start; after the war he is said to have returned but, having seen the devastation of his farm, he immediately left again. His were the possessions identified during the excavation of the crater lip in 2007.

The owner then authorised the grandfather of the present farmer's wife to clear, level and restore the land to cultivation and to reconstruct the farm, and granted him tenancy of the farm's 23 hectares. He was then a young farmer, just back from the war and newly married with a small child. While reconstructing the farm, he and his wife lived in temporary housing between St Yvon and Plugstreet where their first child was born; by 1924, when their second child (father of the current lady of the house) was born, they were installed in a new farm reconstructed close to the original one. The location of the original

COTTAGE AND SHELTERS

MOATED FARM,

farm, dominated by a massive mine crater still visible today, was turned into a pond surrounded by pasture, covering land that had always been poor and waterlogged and was now also riddled with war debris; it is of little surprise that the modern farmer wished to improve it by redistributing the crater lip.

Like the pre-war farm, the new one consisted of three main buildings but no longer had a moat and it was closer to the road: as in many other neighbouring farms, reconstruction had been a chance to improve and modernise. Once reconstruction was completed, the pre-war tenant made an unsuccessful attempt to reclaim the tenancy, which remained with the present family who some years ago bought the farm. As fate would have it, the pre-war tenant's great-grandchild married into the current owners' family so that his great-great-grandchild now stands to inherit the

farm, perhaps a final moment of post-war reconstruction of this farm. As the farmer put it when he related this, 'History is truly formidable!'

Received memories of the wartime are not only about reconstruction but also about losses, both material and human. One story related by an interviewee tells of a cache of gold coins (Louis d'Or), buried during the war under a certain tree near the farm at St Yvon and never retrieved again in a devastated landscape

BELOW *'Le Hutte, Messines, near Ploegsteert Wood, March 1917.' In the foreground are the remnants of a barbed wire fence and immediately behind, a small wagon loaded with logs rests on a rail track. Ruined buildings are in the background. The artist, Major Edwin Summerhayes, who was originally an architect in Perth, Western Australia, served with the 44th Battalion on the Western Front. His battalion rested at Ploegsteert Wood before the Battle of Messines.* From a pen and ink watercolour by Edwin Summerhayes/AWM ART03550

TAKEN from ST. YVES towards GERMAN TRENCHES

where all landmarks had been obliterated. More poignantly people today still recall individual human losses: for instance a cousin's grandfather 'hit by the first shell fired in the war' while standing in a field with two of his children, and who died a few days later 'on the very day his wife gave birth in the cellar where she was sheltering from the bombardments'; or paternal grandparents both 'killed by Germans' in unclear circumstances, leaving behind four young orphans, one of whom later died 'of poverty and misery'.

People can still name and enumerate those who died fighting in the war and those who returned safely, both in their own family and also in those of their friends and neighbours. Almost a century on, the First World War is still clearly recognised as an event shaping local genealogies and families. The impact of war also infuses local understandings of the landscape as, for example, when a man explained that the twists and turns in the roads

around St Yvon were due to the occurrence of shell-holes that the road-builders had to avoid. True or false, this claim reveals the perception of a landscape radically shaped by war. Similarly, residents are clearly aware of 'gaps' created by war destruction in the local landscape and built environment, such as the location of the many 'châteaux' (bourgeois houses) belonging to landowners and industrialists, now known only through pre-war photos that many locals collect.

These losses are not necessarily blamed on the Germans: indeed, one man said that after the First World War Germans had often returned people's belongings that they had come across, hidden in or around houses. In his own family's case, some items taken from his grandparents' house (later destroyed) were returned by the grandchild of an officer who had been billeted there, and who had recently sent back a family genealogy and photos he had made of the house and garden: 'so

PLOEGSTEERT CHURCH

PLOEGSTEERT VILLAGE

I was able to see my grandmother's garden, that I had never seen …. People say that the Germans destroyed and pillaged everything in '14, but they weren't too bad.'

Even though the civilian experience was and is not publicly memorialised and it is relatively little studied by comparison to the military aspects of the First World War, it is a rich and complex period of history that almost a century after the conflict still leaves traces in the former battlefields. Like the board game passed down from grandmother to child, grandchild and great-grandchild, objects and stories from that time linger among local inhabitants, infusing their understanding of local history, identity and place.

Out of the Ashes

Factory Farm had been both home and business, but not only had the land been devastated by being on the front line for four

years; it had been the site of two mine attacks. As previously described, one had rent farmland asunder and the other had obliterated the farm itself, together with the barns, stables, and workshops. The scene of family life had utterly vanished from the landscape, leaving only a watery pool with the lip around it. If the pain of departure was dreadful then the pain of return was different but no less awful.

However, the archaeological remains show that many people were not going to be defeated by the appalling scene that greeted them. Toward the northern end of the excavations one area in particular gives evidence of the determination of the Belgians to rebuild their lives. Geophysical survey in 2007 showed distinct anomalies at the northern end of a wooded paddock, where there was a distinct depression in the soil. A trench was opened to investigate this and soon a large area of concrete rubble was encountered. Gradually this was removed and the remains

RIGHT *The corrugated iron revetting sheets of the British front line positions just east of the sunken lane at St Yvon. It was from here that the Australians went over the top on the morning of 7 June.*

of a German bunker were revealed. It had a thick concrete floor and the remains of its walls, reinforced with iron bars, standing about 30cm high. The walls had been broken and the reinforcing bars cut off. Yet there was no trace of this ironwork and the remaining concrete rubble was not sufficient to be the entire remains of the position, suggesting salvage. The work on the destruction of the bunker appeared too methodical to be the result of battle damage, or of demolition by military engineers to deny the position to the enemy, should they return. The removal of the reinforcing bars and of much of the concrete indicated that other processes were at work.

Moreover, few military artefacts were recovered during excavations, save for a few cartridges and a German stick grenade that could be the result of routine battlefield clearance. This all pointed to civilian, rather than military, activity and so suggests an event in the reconstruction of the landscape. The removal of the bunker could have been carried out during two specific phases: initially the local people took it upon themselves to remove certain structures as part of their own reclamation of their land but, later on,

following the payment of war reparations by Germans, the Belgian government sent out itinerant gangs of labourers to demolish such structures. The work gangs would call at farms and ask whether there were blockhouses for removal. If they were refused the farmer was given a document to say that he had refused and now had no further claim on state assistance. However, some bunkers had, by this time, been given over to other uses and even today some still serve as cattle byres, hay stores, chicken coops, and tool sheds.

This raised the question as to which phase of works had seen the demolition of this particular bunker; one specific discovery offered a clue to the answer. Among the rubble a ceramic stopper from a beer bottle was found. The top of the cap said this was a product of the De Simpel Brewery in Warneton, a few miles south. Warneton is the town to which St Yvon looks; although Messines is closer it is a Flemish, rather than Walloon settlement and so the residents of the Walloon enclave of St Yvon and Ploegsteert traditionally seemed to have looked south for goods and services, including beer. It is likely that the people demolishing the bunker were refreshing themselves with their own local brew.

However, this interpretation is supported by the fact that the reinforcing bars and much of the concrete rubble had been salvaged, indeed the rubble had also all been broken down into manageable lumps that were much the same size as modern hardcore. As the natives of St Yvon returned they had to rebuild the roads and houses of the commune and they needed money but had no fields on which to raise crops. What there was to hand was scrap metal that could be sold on or reused and, from the bunkers that reinforced the German lines, came a ready source of hardcore for road surfacing. Careful inspection of the edges of the lanes in the area reveals chunks of good-quality German concrete acting as foundations to the modern tarmac. Enquiries with the farmer supported this interpretation of an early post-war civilian demolition and reuse. He was adamant that he had not been responsible for

the demolition and had not even been aware of the bunker's presence, suggesting that no one had mentioned it either to him or to his wife, whose family had owned the land.

Not all of these bunkers were destroyed after the war; a number served as replacement buildings for those destroyed on farms and in villages in the years of fighting. Some of these imposing structures were integral to the story of the Battle of Messines. One of these bunkers, a three-chambered construction with arched roof on the western edge of the Ploegsteert Wood still survives, behind the modern house of one of the members of the local History Society. This concrete construction – now used as a shed with many rusted objects – was a site of much pain in the Battle of Messines, as Australian casualties were brought back here to be treated. Evidence for a humanity not always highlighted by studies of the war can be seen: traced into the wet concrete render covering one of the shelter's

BELOW *A bunker on the edge of Ploegsteert Wood. This was an Australian Advanced Dressing Station (ADS) on 7 June and, as such, would have been a scene of much suffering.*

RIGHT *A Maxim gun round, still retaining part of the belt, excavated beside the Factory Farm crater. This may well have been part of the ammunition taken up by machine gun teams after the mine explosions on 7 June.*

outside walls is the image of a man's torso. It seems to be a depiction of an officer. There is no indication of the artist or of his model and yet nonetheless this image provides a direct link to the men of the Allied armies that fought here. As such, this image and the bunker itself – obvious traces of a war that was so damaging to a village – are now seen as elements that should be preserved as part of the history of that reconstructed landscape.

In addition to the demolition of the bunker excavated in 2007, other structures have vanished, including the blockhouse overturned by the Ultimo crater, and almost all trace of the trenches as they have been filled in and returned to agriculture. However, excavation of the trenches shows how the former battlefields were cleared, whether by labour gangs or locals.

The upper layers of the fills of each excavated trench show a mixed collection of battlefield debris, including shell splinters, unexploded munitions, and bundles of barbed wire that appear to have been cleared from the fields. In addition, some excavation results show signs of salvage. For example, in the sap dug into the western side of the lip of the Ultimo crater there were traces of wood from the revetting of the trench, but this had been largely removed and the XPM (expanded metal sheeting), a form of heavy duty mesh, had been removed from its frames, roughly rolled and dumped back into the sap before its final backfilling. While this could have been military salvage, since the feature had become a dump before its filling, one suspects that XPM might have been of more use to the soldiers, rather than to civilians seeking building materials or firewood.

The scale and speed of reconstruction and the Flamand determination of the locals to rebuild their lives after the war can be seen on the lane that runs between the excavation areas, where the earliest standing building in the area dates to 1921, less than three years after the end of the war. It demonstrates the desire of the returning population to bring life back to some sense of normality, although the landscape around would still have been heavily scarred. Reconstruction still continues today. As we have seen, the fields around the Factory Farm crater have recently been improved, using redistributed earth thrown up by the mine. In 1920 this would have been a significant undertaking but in the days of machinery it became a simpler job. As occurred often during the reconstruction period, human remains were recovered. Given that human remains had been unearthed when the lip was disturbed it seemed sensible to undertake further investigations in order to see whether all had been recovered and whether any context could be discerned for the burials. The area where the bodies were discovered was excavated in extreme detail to recover any bones left.

A 9m² area was gridded and each square metre was subjected to fingertip search, with even the topsoil being searched. In the end only one foot bone was found, demonstrating that the local, amateur archaeologists had already done a thorough job. This single bone was later added to the mass grave at the VDK cemetery in Langemarck, where the bodies had been laid to rest following the original discoveries. No context for the burials could be discerned, suggesting that they had been concealed by soil from the crater. In addition, few finds were recovered save for a 1917 dated 7.92 German cartridge. Around this was the fabric and copper from the belt that would have been used to feed rounds through a Maxim gun, which led to the interpretation that these men were part of the machine-gun teams ordered into the crater to enfilade the Australian attackers, as they crossed no-man's-land toward the German line in their attempt to take and fortify the Ultimo crater.

Listening to the Land

Some cultures believe that stories make the landscape and that they are the ancestral memory of the people. This project shows that those told by both the land and the people do make places unto unique locations. Here, one small section of an enormous battlefront has given up its stories to be passed on and contributed to the narratives of remembrance that create networks around the globe.

Another such story is that told to the excavators by Claude, owner of the Auberge opposite the Ploegsteert Memorial. When he was a boy Claude knew an old woman who had been a child herself at the outbreak of war. The Ghurkhas arrived as part of the Indian Army and had been billeted in the area. They had taken the little girl – who was fascinated by the small, dark soldiers – under their wing, and played with her. Before they moved on and she, in turn, left as a refugee, they had given her a present to seal their friendship. She told Claude that it was a necklace made of smoked German ears taken as trophies in nearby fighting. The story epitomises the human experience of war, of dislocation, loss, and of odd moments of humanity coupled with horror: the land, the objects and the stories endure as the last witnesses.

[1] 33rd Battalion Official History, 46.
[2] Walle, 1978: 462, 473.
[3] Walle, Ibid.: 465.
[4] Cf. Clout, 1996: 11.

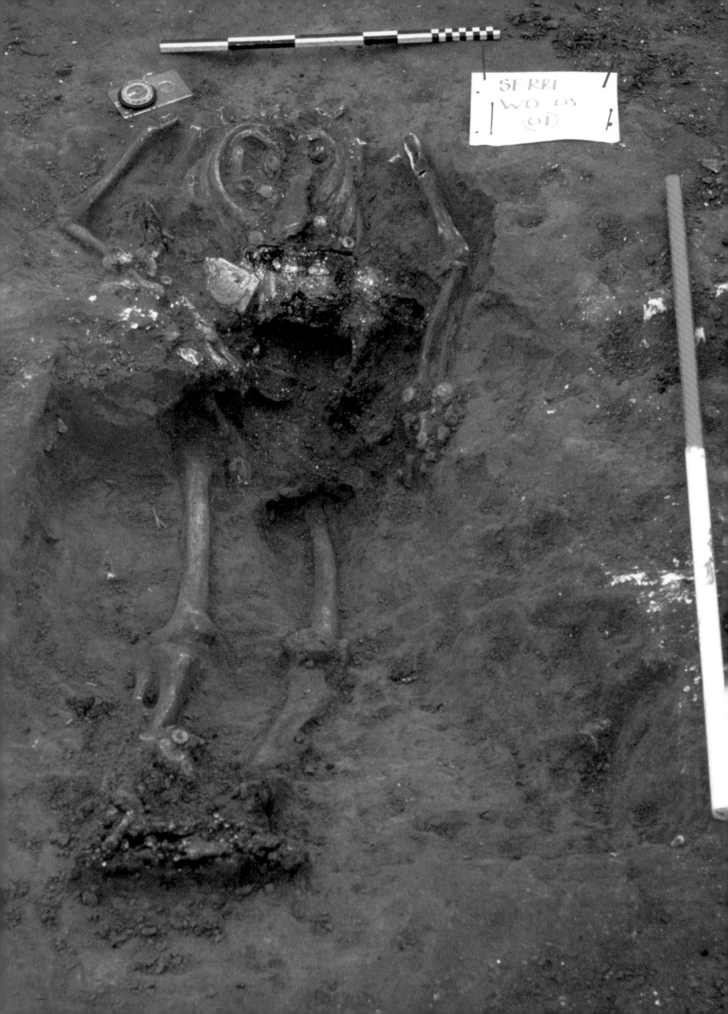

SERRE
WO OS
(OD)

CHAPTER 9

The Unknown Soldier

The Menin Gate in the Belgian town of Ypres is perhaps one of the most powerful monuments in the world – one derided by the war poet Siegfried Sassoon as being a 'sepulchre of crime'. On its arched walls are carved the names of over 54,000 men, men of the British Empire who were killed in the First World War in Belgium and whose remains were never recovered. Some had been buried in graves that were forgotten as the passage of war moved on; some were hastily placed in shell-holes or disused trenches; some simply vanished, being 'knocked to spots' by artillery or being covered by or sucked down into the mud. These were men from all around the world – Britain, South Africa, New Zealand, India, and Australia. Above each of the central arches is inscribed:

TO THE ARMIES
OF THE BRITISH EMPIRE
WHO STOOD HERE
FROM 1914 TO 1918
AND TO THOSE OF THEIR DEAD
WHO HAVE NO KNOWN GRAVE

When examining the Menin Gate, the commander of the Messines campaign, Lord Plumer, discussed the fate of all those men who had no known grave. He told families that the monument was a fitting one to commemorate their sacrifice and that in grieving for their loved ones that had been posted as missing that, in fact, 'He is not missing; he is here.'

In recent years, individuals have made

several discoveries of bodies on First World War sites in and around the Ploegsteert region. These include the body of Private Harry Wilkinson of the 2nd Battalion Lancashire Fusiliers who was killed in November 1914 and re-buried at Prowse Point cemetery in October 2000;[1] and that of Private Richard Lancaster, also of the 2nd Battalion Lancashire Fusiliers, who disappeared on 10 November 1914 and whose remains were recovered to the south of the study area in 2006, being reburied in 2007.[2]

In 2003–4, directly within the confines of the project study area, the remains of two German soldiers were found. They were located within the upcast of the Factory Farm mine and were associated with a series of artefacts, including machine-gun belt ammunition (for the MG08 gun), a Luger, a comb and (most importantly) the remnants of an identity disc. On discussions with the *Volksbund Deutsche Kriegsgräberfürsorge* (VDK) the finders were able to identify one of the men as being *Unteroffizier* Julius Wilhelm Brugger of the 2nd Company of the 5th Bavarian Regiment, born on 2 January 1894 and killed by the explosion of the mine (or in the capture of the crater) on 7 June 1917, the start of the Battle of Messines.[3] Both men were subsequently reinterred at Langemarck.

On 5 August 2008, the archaeology team at St Yvon found the remains of one of the missing Australian soldiers named on the Menin Gate. The following is his story.

The results of the geophysical survey of the battlefield were most revealing; although much

OPPOSITE *The body of German infantryman Jakob Hones, found on the Somme in 2003 by the No-Man's-Land Archaeology team. He was buried wearing his belt order.*

of the German line at St Yvon was obscured by trees or had a quantity of material dumped over it, there were still elements which seemed clear. A section of trench that was far enough north of the Ultimo crater to have avoided the worst of the mine blast, had not been entirely obliterated by the Allied artillery barrage. According to documentary sources, Australian infantry and pioneers had found the damage to the German front line to be so severe that 'turning round the line' was next to impossible. Indeed, this is

what we had found in other areas, especially those closest to the mines. On the survey, this one segment still appeared to have firebays and the crenulated appearance familiar from aerial photographs of the front line, and so it was here that we sited one of the excavation trenches.

Soon, important finds started to appear: the sole of a boot, the side lugs of a pickelhaube, spent Mauser cases, and large strands of German barbed wire. Then another boot was found and yet another. These were soon seen

to still contain the feet and legs of a soldier. As is standard procedure, work was then stopped for the find to be reported to the local police and subsequently to the Belgian Army and the Commonwealth War Graves Commission. The Royal Procurator and Police agreed that our excavation team was to be given permission to recover the remains of the soldier on behalf of the Belgian Army and so, over the next five days we set about the process of excavating the body and the associated artefacts, applying conservation techniques to the latter to ensure the best possible chance of obtaining an identity for the man at a later stage.

Although not setting out to discover human remains, it is an imperative that any fieldwork project in this region has the means to excavate a soldier's body with all the requisite forensic techniques, treating the remains of the man with the utmost dignity at all times. Although the skull, vertebrae and right arm had been disturbed, the vast majority of the man's remains were still present and were recovered. This work was painstaking and done with great care – indeed we took a number of days over the process to ensure that everything was done correctly. Sadly it is not uncommon for sites of this nature to be looted if they are left unattended, and so the team mounted round-the-clock guards to ensure that the site was protected.

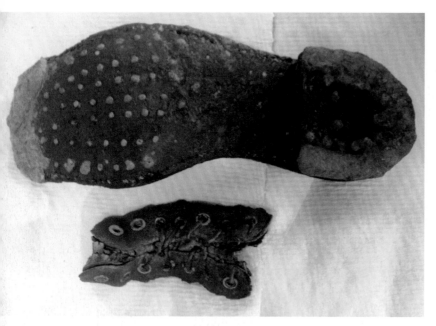

A Corner of a Foreign Field

All facts pertaining to the body are worth noting, as these all contribute to the narrative of the man's life and death and to attempts to obtain an identity for him. So what then could we say about the context in which this man lay? The first striking fact was that the remains of the soldier were found so close to the surface – the remains of his right arm being only about 40cm below the modern ground surface – and this had led to part of this arm and the man's skull being disturbed by plough actions as the area is once again farmland. His feet, still in their British-pattern boots, lay at a level some 20cm below his skull and were thus undisturbed.

The body was situated around 1m to the east of the German front line trench (which became the new Australian line at St Yvon after the attacks of 7 June) lying roughly east–west with his back to the north and his head at the eastern end. He lay on his left side, his right leg over his left, with his knees drawn up towards his chest and with his left hand still around the stock of his Lee Enfield rifle. There was German barbed wire, Allied shrapnel balls and several fired Mauser cases around him, the normal detritus of the battlefield. We could also see that he was not in a grave cut of any sort and there were no

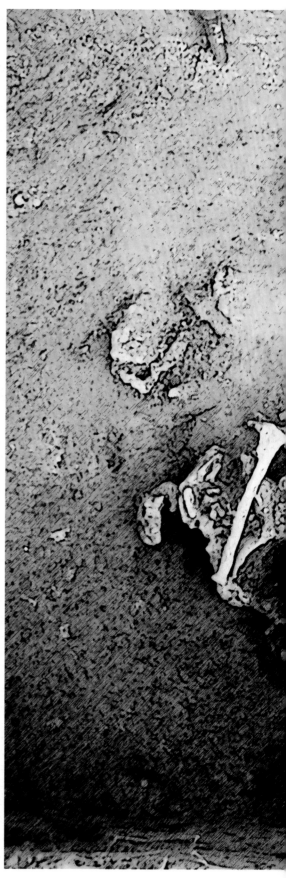

signs of any material having been removed from his body. There was also nothing that gave immediate clarity as to how the man died, although by the very fact that pretty much all of his skeleton was present and articulated would suggest that this man was certainly not one of the many thousands who was hit directly by shellfire. He was found in the centre of the positions in the line attacked by the 33rd Battalion, 9th Brigade, Australian 3rd Division that fateful morning.

The context of his burial does, however, suggest he was killed immediately after having passed the German front line, whereupon he was covered by spoil thrown up by blast. Having taken the battlefield, the Australians did whatever they could to recover their fallen comrades and this man had certainly not been buried by comrades or enemies; there was neither commemoration nor reverence in his burial. There was also no archaeological evidence for a grave cut of any sort. Being covered by material thrown up by shell blast might explain why his body could not be recovered.

John Laffin, although not using any recognisable archaeological recording did at least consider the deposition context of remains when he encountered them. At Bullecourt in France he pondered over the finding of the remains of an Australian soldier which he referred to as the 'Bullecourt Digger':

The absence of a personal weapon, steel helmet and grenades points to a battlefield burial by mates, who would not have buried such valuable equipment; indeed they were under orders not to do so. The men took any grenades for their own use while Salvage Corps men picked up discarded equipment, which was repaired and reissued. It seems unlikely that the Bullecourt Digger was buried by shellbursts covering him in dirt and debris. Most soldiers who had been overwhelmed in this manner usually had a weapon with them, notably the bayonet on their belt, or grenades in their pockets when their remains were recovered from the battlefield in the years after the war.[4]

This would seem to be important for the remains of the man found in our excavations, as all of these elements of equipment were still with him as we shall see.

From the battlefield debris around the body (Mauser cases, shrapnel balls, wire, tile) and the level in which it lay, he may well have been in one of the earlier assault companies in the attacks of 7 June, lying in a slight scrape or shell-crater in the back of the German trench, and was covered by shell-blast material from the destroyed German trench, and subsequently by material cut from the German trench when 3rd Division turned the line round and added the firestep which we found in our excavations.

The fact that his body lay with feet at a greater depth than head, despite being in the vicinity of the parados of the German trench, can be explained by the fact that the back of the German front line had been heavily damaged both by the shock wave of the mine blast (in some regions) and by the artillery barrage which followed. Our evidence showed this to be the case throughout the German front line. Indeed, the attacking Australians that had been ordered to 'turn round' the German front-line positions in the early stages of the battle found this quite impossible in several areas, as these positions had simply been obliterated; thus they had to start afresh, and used corrugated iron and expanded metal (XPM) to achieve this. Although the geophysical survey results indicated that this was one of the more intact areas of German fire-trench – and undeniably there was no re-fortifying with corrugated iron – this trench had still been heavily damaged by Allied actions.

Equipment

A useful starting point in this discussion might be an examination of the orders issued to members of the 9th Brigade (and hence to the Australian 33rd Battalion among others) with regard to equipment that the men of each company were told to take with them into the attacks of 7 June, as this might provide clues as to the duties of the man we had found. Although one must be careful not to assume that soldiers always followed these instructions faithfully, for the

most part they provide a very good indicator. 'A flurried rush and we're at our jumping-off tape line, thankfully dropping down to seek what little cover we can find and grabbing for our water bottles. We carry two each and have orders that no water is to be touched until we are on our objective. ..'[5] The memoirs of one particular Australian infantryman involved in the battle do illustrate that these instructions (see x below) were important:

Orders to the 33rd Btn for the attack of 7 June
Secret:
33rd BATTALION, AIF.
Instructions for Forthcoming Operations No 1.

Equipment. 1.
(i).   All officers taking part in the attack will be dressed and equipped the same as the men. Sticks will not be carried.
(ii).   Rifle and bayonets will be carried by all ranks except No 1 Lewis Gunners who will have revolvers. All ranks will wear web equipment less the pack. Officers will carry revolvers in addition to the rifle and bayonet.

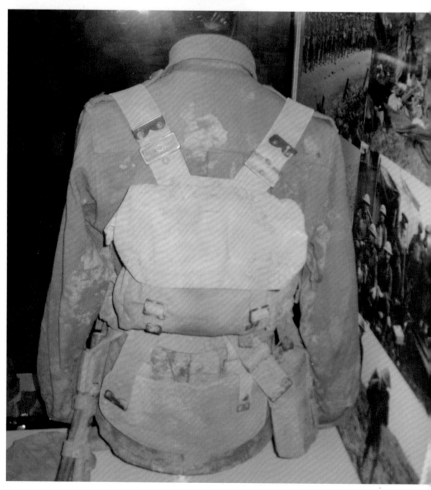

ABOVE *The components of the small box respirator found with the body of the Australian soldier.*

BELOW *A close-up of the respirator tube undergoing conservation work after excavation.*

(iii). The haversack will be worn on the back and will contain 48 hours rations, spare oil tin and cardigan jacket, the waterproof sheet will be placed under the flags of the haversack. Lewis gunners will wear the haversack on the left side.

(iv). The mess tin and cover will be slung outside the haversack and will contain the grocery ration and the unexpanded day's ration. Lewis Gunners will carry the mess tin on the waist belt at the back.

(v). Each man will carry four sandbags on his back under neath [sic] the supporting straps.

(vi). Ammunition will be carried as follows: (a). Bayonet men – 170 rounds. (b). Lewis gunners, bombers and Rifle Grenadiers 120 rounds. (c). Signallers, Runners and Carriers – 50 rounds.

(vii). All ranks except runners will carry two Mills Grenades one in each top pocket. These bombs are not to be used by the individual except in cases of emergency, but are to be collected at Objective Dumps.

(viii). Each man in B, C, and D Cos will carry one aeroplane flare in his lower right pocket. One flare per two men will be carried by A Company less carriers and runners. The Battalion Reserve will not carry flares. These flares are to be collected at Objective Dumps.

(ix). Box respirators will be worn at the 'ALERT'.

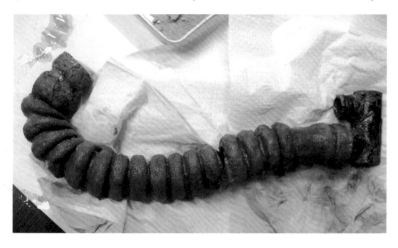

(x).   Water bottles will be filled. The necessity of conserving water cannot be too strongly impressed on all ranks.

(xi).   Each platoon in C and D Companies – A. Company's 'crater' platoon, and the two platoons forming the first wave of D. Company will carry across 15 shovels and 3 picks. Each man in A Company, less the 'crater' platoon and moppers-up and each man in the second wave of B Company will carry either pick or shovel in ratio of 3 shovels to 1 pick. The tools will be carried on the back under the haversack and belt. When D Company is mentioned it will include the "crater" platoon of A Company from the date of issue of these instructions.

(xii).   Lewis gunners, except No 1. will carry six magazines each.

(xiii). The bombing sections will carry bombs as follows: Throwers – 10 bombs. Carriers – 15 bombs. Bayonet men – 5 bombs. Bombs will be carried in a bag on the left side.

(xiv).   Rifle grenadiers will carry 6 rifle grenades, 6 spare rods and 5 spare blank cartridges – all to be in a sandbag at left side.

(xv).   Wire cutters will be carried by first wave.

(xvi).   Twelve S.O.S. rockets will be carried by each company.

(xvii). Mopping-up parties will carry tear bombs.

Spare Kits, Packs, etc.

Greatcoat and spare kit will be stowed in packs which must be clearly marked with number, rank and name of owner. Small articles of personal property must not be placed in pockets of greatcoats. Attention to this will avoid loss if it becomes necessary to issue greatcoats. These kits will be stored at Quartermaster's store by noon on the day preceeding zero day.

Badges

(i).   A patch of white cloth will be sewn to the back of the right sleeve above the elbow. A Company, less one platoon, will have an additional patch sewn on below the one already mentioned.

(ii).   In addition to the above badges, specialists and carrying parties will wear distinguishing colour bands 1½in wide on the left forearm as follows:

Scouts	Green bands.
Runners	Red "
Carrying Parties	Yellow "
Mopping Up	White "
Salvage	khaki band with 'salvage' in red letters.

(iii).   Regimental and Company Signallers will wear blue bands on shoulder straps.

(iv).   Men equipped with wire cutters or wire breakers will wear a piece of white tape tied to the shoulder strap.

Documents and Maps

(i).   All ranks taking part in the assault are forbidden to take letters, papers, orders, or sketches which, if captured, would give information to the enemy.

(ii).   Officers may carry maps of enemy trenches, or sketches showing particular areas in enemy ground, but these must not contain any information concerning our objectives or disposition. [6]

BELOW *General Service Shovel found by the archaeological team.*

As expected, our excavations not only revealed the presence of the remains of a soldier, but he was accompanied by a huge quantity of military items and personal equipment. The well-preserved artefacts associated with the body added to the narrative surrounding the man and told more of his story. Our first glimpse of the man was of his boots. These were certainly not jackboots, although German soldiers moved away from wearing these later in the war as this footwear was liable to come off, thanks to the suction of the mud of Flanders and Wallonia. Given the fact that the soldier was found by a German trench,

with many Mauser cartridges and fragments of German barbed wire around him, it might have been reasonable to assume that he was a German, particularly when our first view of any insignia was that of the badge of Hesse on a pickelhaube with him.

However, it soon became apparent from webbing and remnants of khaki that the soldier was wearing uniform and equipment consistent with that of the British Empire infantryman post-1915. All evidence also pointed to the fact that he was not an officer. Although, sadly, he retained no Divisional insignia, it was clear that this man was an Australian soldier; he had the remnants of corduroy trousers, two in-situ Australian collar badges, and one in situ Australian shoulder title. Further to this, he had another Australian shoulder title (with both split-pins in the same eyelet) in his small pack on his back (or in his pocket); this find was made more powerful for the excavation team as it was made only a day after a briefing from one of the excavation supervisors, Steve Roberts, who explained that this practice was not uncommon among the infantry of the First World War to prevent loss of such items. The correct

procedure for wearing infantry webbing was for shoulder straps to be worn below the epaulet straps; however, many infantrymen found it easier to wear them over, as this would make it easier to remove the webbing. The problem with this methodology was that the webbing straps could snag on the shoulder titles when being put on or taken off – by removing the shoulder titles, this alleviated the problem.

Intriguingly, our soldier's helmet was placed under his hip with the strap up over the brim as though fastened to his pack, as in standard marching order. The hollow (interior) of the helmet was against the man's hip and it seems unlikely that the helmet could fall or roll into this position when the man fell, nor could it be ploughed into this area at a later stage, even with the strap over the brim.

The man's nationality had implications both for the procedures followed by the excavation team and also for the potential for later identification. In addition to calls to the Commonwealth War Graves Commission, numerous Australian officials in Canberra, London and Brussels had to be informed that one of their missing soldiers had been found. It should perhaps be noted that many of those who fought in the Australian ranks in the First World War had only relatively recently moved to that country, either as emigrants from various European countries or as migrant temporary labourers. Thus there was the possibility that the man we had found had in fact been born in Europe before being adopted by a new nation.

What They Carried

The man was found in full battle order, he had nothing to indicate that he might be an officer, and had no elements of uniform that might indicate that he was here in the colder months of the year – he had no woollens, no coat. The insignia he carried did not include the telltale oval patch of the 3rd Division, which might have revealed both Division and Battalion, nor were there any patches of sewn cloth that might have illustrated the particular duty he was to perform in the attack in which he fell. It might be useful here to itemise the sheer quantity of finds made with the remains of the man.

LEFT *The 'Brodie' helmet used by soldiers of the British Empire after 1916.*

BELOW *The interior of the helmet after its liner had been removed for conservation. Note the strap and buckle toward the top left of the helmet and the fact that this was looped up over the outer brim.*

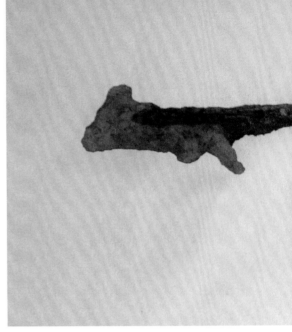

An inventory of elements of uniform

■ Leather soles and uppers of both boots still with the hobnails, toe and heel plates, and with laces still threaded through the seven eyelets of the uppers.

■ Fragments of socks.

■ Fragments of underpants.

■ Poppers from his braces.

■ The khaki collars of his uniform.

■ Shoulder epaulette and button with the standard map of Australia on the latter.

■ Corduroy trouser fragments.

■ Two 'Australia' shoulder titles (though one was held in his small pack or pocket).

■ A large quantity of webbing, pouches and buckles.

■ Two 'rising sun' collar badges.

LEFT, TOP An epaulette button bearing the map of Australia, typical of that worn by an Australian infantryman. Thanks to the metal of the button, the khaki uniform also survived well.

LEFT, MIDDLE One of the many webbing buckles found as part of the soldier's equipment.

LEFT, BOTTOM The gas goggles recovered with the Australian. Both glass eye-pieces are still intact.

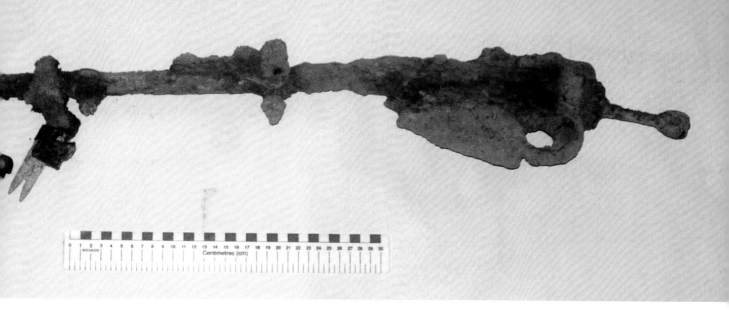

An inventory of equipment.

- PH gas helmet.
- Small box respirator and bag.
- Gas goggles.
- Short Magazine Lee Enfield rifle (including its oil bottle, pull-through, steel disc and butt plate) with part of the rifle strap, though the majority of the wooden parts had rotted away.
- Many charger clips with ammunition (5 rounds) in pouches. Each pouch held two chargers.
- At least one No 5 Mills bomb (this was found associated with the man's skull).
- Brodie helmet (including the remants of the liner) found beneath pelvis and with the chinstrap looped over the helmet brim.

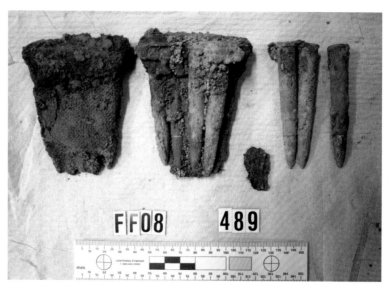

TOP *Short Magazine Lee Enfield (SMLE) rifle of the British infantryman. The Australian soldier was still holding this in death.*

RIGHT, MIDDLE *A detail of the rifle strap showing two rounds placed in a loop to prevent the strap slipping. This sort of knowledge would only have been acquired on campaign and thus indicated a soldier with some degree of experience.*

RIGHT, BOTTOM *Some of the many .303 rounds, still in their charger clips, found in the pouches of the soldier.*

- Two iodine ampoules of medical kit with the liquid still contained within them.
- A possible broken morphine ampoule.
- The entrenching tool and its wooden handle.
- The bayonet, with its tip broken off, and leather scabbard.
- Water canteen.
- Mess kit including spoon, razor and pocket knife.
- Small pack.
- Large pack.
- Food tins in small pack (shown as rusted fragments, not retrievable).

LEFT, TOP *Much of the medical kit with the infantryman was still intact. Here we see three phials, the two at the front still hold the iodine which could have been used to sterilise wounds before the application of a field dressing.*

LEFT, MIDDLE *An entrenching tool found by the lower back of the soldier.*

BELOW, LEFT *The tip of the bayonet recovered had broken off.*

BELOW *This detail of the leather scabbard of the bayonet shows the stitching. It was clear that the bayonet was not in its sheath when the soldier was killed.*

What is also significant in this collection is what was *not* found with the man; this information is potentially important when examining the secret attack orders for the Australian brigades at the Battle of Messines, as these detail equipment to be carried by the various companies. Would this information be useful in assisting attempts at identification, or would it reveal that the troops simply did not carry all the items they were supposed to; that in fact archaeology can be perhaps more useful in informing us of the actualities of battle than the documents that proclaim the ideal situation. With the amount of equipment found, and the care of excavation, no items were left behind once the archaeological work was complete.

As seen, the orders for the 9th Brigade were for wire cutters to be carried by all members of companies in the first attacking wave; none were retrieved at St Yvon. Furthermore, no gas grenades were recovered, a requirement for soldiers in mopping-up parties, though some were present in the surrounding field. Perhaps more significant was the fact that no buttons from the front of the soldier's tunic were found. The man had not had items souveniered from his body, and we also know that soil conditions were such that uniform buttons would survive, as we found one from the epaulet; copper alloy items were preserved well. There is a possibility therefore that the absence of these buttons might well be connected to the death of the Australian soldier.

BELOW Still in situ prior to its excavation with the Australian soldier and the rest of his equipment was the standard blue water bottle of the British infantryman.

An inventory of items of personal possession

▪ *Wallet with French francs, some dated 1916.*
▪ *A pickelhaube in his back pack.*
▪ *Toothbrush (marked France Flexadent).*
▪ *Personal issue pen knife.*
▪ *Personal issue 'ID tag', corroded and broken into three pieces. This was taken to the University of Ghent for analysis, but to no avail.*

After battles of the First World War, no matter how successful their outcome, the necessity for burial details was inevitable. Plans were established at Battalion level to facilitate this sad duty. The 33rd Battalion of the Australian 3rd Division had just such a set of orders, orders which also included elements on how troops should report on the fate of soldiers that were deemed 'missing'. Battalion pioneers were to

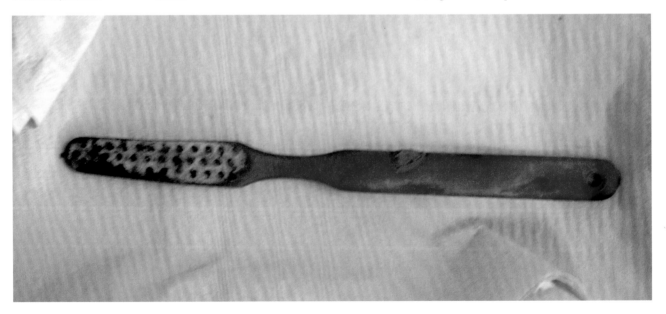

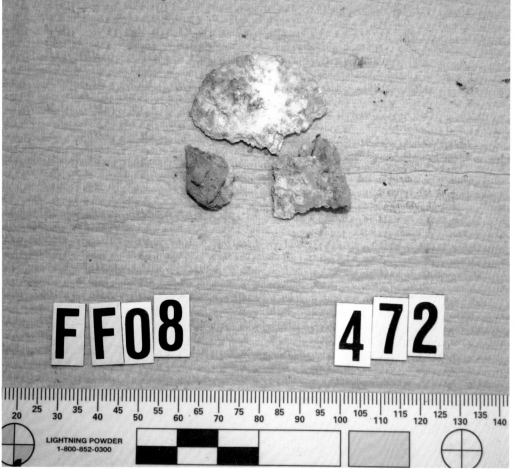

ABOVE *This pocket knife was found in positions cut through the destroyed German lines by the Australians and is typical of those issued to soldiers.*

LEFT *One deep frustration for the team was that although the Australian had a metal identity disc (presumably a private purchase) with him, it was far too corroded to retain any information, even with x-ray analysis.*

RIGHT *A military funeral at a cemetery at Poperinghe, Belgium, on 11 August 1917.* IWM Q5875

dig graves for the dead, and regimental burial officers and chaplains were also required.

The official procedures for burial of the dead involved:

- *Burial of the dead of our own Forces, of our Allies, and of the enemy.*
- *Collection and disposal of their effects.*
- *Registration of graves.*
- *The importance of carrying out this work expeditiously and systematically cannot too strongly be emphasised. The Division will be responsible for all burials within the area.*

The duties of officers in charge of burial parties was 'to systematically search the area for dead; to collect the dead as situations offered and to place them in areas little opposed to artillery fire, at least 100m from houses and not near a well or water supply; to collect personal items and id discs in ration or other suitable bags, to mark them and hand them to HQ of unit concerned green identity discs to be buried with the body. Bodies of our own forces, of our allies and of the enemy collected separately and buried in separate trenches.'[7]

To ensure identification the graves of each group were marked with a metal disc or standard bearing divisional sign and numbers. It was acknowledged that:

during periods of heavy fighting, the disposal of the dead and the marking of graves becomes a difficult problem. Burials have to be carried out at night or during a lull in the fighting, and it frequently happens that a unit is withdrawn without being able to bury any of those killed in action, in which case the in-going unit will undertake the work of burying the dead.

Personnel reported missing, or wounded and missing, during offensive operations:

- *Units will be informed by Anzac Section, 3rd Echelon, of all negative information on hand, viz:*

Advice that the man does not appear on an official Prisoners of War List, that there is no record of his admission to Hospital subsequent to the date of his being reported missing, no record of any information at Administrative Headquarters.

Of any statement which may have been received, and which may have a bearing on the case

A Court of Enquiry: Courts of Enquiry will be held as directed by Brigade Headquarters. It is essential that these Courts should be dealt with upon the same lines, and that uniform findings should be made. ...[8](Ibid).

The recording of the accounts of soldiers was important and led to some very useful records, in particular for those Australian soldiers who were classed as missing in action: 'The Australian Red Cross Society created the Wounded and Missing Enquiry Bureau for the very purpose of finding out the exact circumstances of the death of as many Australians killed or missing in action as possible. They achieved this mainly by searching for living witnesses of a deceased soldier's final moments.'[9] Such records were helpful in attempts to identify the soldier found by our excavation; some records noted at least rudimentary efforts at burial, or retrieval of artefacts from the bodies of some of the slain. However, this was not something that happened to the Plugstreet soldier, and so the men in these records could be ruled out as candidates in the identification process.

Known unto God

In spite of all the procedures noted above, there was an inevitability that not all the bodies of men killed in battle would be recovered at the time, and so there were huge moves to try to retrieve at least some of these remains following the end of the war.

In the early 1920s there were Exhumation Companies under British command in Flanders and northern France within the

LEFT *An unidentified soldier views the Australian graves along the old OG1 (Old German) line on the battlefield of Pozières, 16 September 1917. All these graves have been marked and recorded by the Graves Registration Section.* AWM E00999

ABOVE *Members of the Graves Registration Detachment, Australian Section, of the Imperial War Graves Unit, load bodies from a mass grave to be put in single graves in 1919. After exhumation the bodies are wrapped in groundsheets with ID tags prior to reburial in permanent war cemeteries. Identified is 3162 Private Herbert James (Bert) Kingston (standing on the wagon). Formerly a member of the 47th Battalion, he enlisted from Bundaberg, Queensland, and sailed with the 8th Reinforcements.* AWM P04541.001

Directorate of Graves Registration and Enquiries. The equipment used by these people was

two pairs of rubber gloves, two spades, a pair of pliers, stakes to mark the graves, tarpaulin and rope to wrap bodies in, stretchers and the dangerous disinfectant cresol. All possible graves on the delineated terrain were first marked out with stakes. This task required a great deal of experience because there were virtually no crosses left. Prominent indications of a possible burial were rat holes dug around the remains, pieces of military gear, sudden concentrations of wild grass (broad and dark sprigs), and blue-grey-black discolouring patterns in the soil.[10]

This was the first real attempt at a forensic recovery of bodies and an endeavour to give a name to the soldier in the reburial process; an attempt to examine artefacts, uniforms

and equipment that had specific details of the individual associated with them.

In a parallel process, the Australian government acknowledged that both the possibility that all of their fallen would be recovered was remote, and that, given the distance of Australia from the theatres of conflict, relatives of the deceased would not be able to visit either the Menin Gate or – of those with an identified place of burial – the graveside. It was incredibly difficult for families of the deceased to be able to tend their grave – something of some small comfort to families in Britain who were at least afforded such opportunities.

In addition to a memorial scroll and plaque, the next-of-kin of Australian soldiers killed in the First World War were sent a publication called 'Where the Australians Rest – a description of the Cemeteries overseas in which Australians including those whose names can never now be known are buried'. This was prepared under the instructions from the Minister of State for Defence (Senator G.F.

Pearce) in 1920. Several of the cemeteries with large numbers of Australians buried within were depicted by woodcuts, others were described. As this was issued shortly after the end of the war, the search for remains of the missing was still under way: 'The authorities have been making every effort that not one soldier whose remains can be found on those old battlefields shall go without a soldier's honourable burial.'

In all too many cases, alas, those who fall upon the field in battle, fall in some part of the field where no friend can reach them alive. The burial parties, which work wherever it is possible, often in danger, cannot reach them, under the machine guns of the enemy. Months afterwards, sometimes years, the battle rolls beyond that place, and these poor forms are dealt with as tenderly as the time and place allow. The officials of the Graves Registration Unit examine carefully each part of the old No Man's Land, and erect a cross, or other symbol, wherever these brave men are found. Often the spot has already been marked by some soldier fixing beside the grave the rifle which lies near it, or laying reverently upon the little mound some shrapnel-torn helmet that may once have belonged to him who lies there. In a few instances, the names of these men are found on their identity discs, or the sodden papers which may sometimes still lie beside them, But too often there is left no trace or clue to the soldier's name. Private or officer, he lies there, 'An Unknown Soldier'.[11]

Although, unlike America with JPAC (Joint Prisoner of War, Missing in Action Accounting Command), Australia, as with Britain, does not have a policy of looking for its war dead; this is one of a number of cases at the moment involving the discovery of the remains of Australian servicemen. The burials of five men at Zonnebeke in Belgium,[12] the mass grave at Fromelles in France, and of Second World War bodies from Papua New Guinea, are all recent discoveries and highlight public demand in Australia to undertake a recovery process or, at the very least, to explore all possibilities for an identification when chance discoveries are made.

The uncovering of the soldier's body on the Plugstreet excavations was unusual for the First World War as he was found on the battlefield, exactly where he had fallen some 90 years ago, and was in full kit, carrying artefacts that gave this man a story, a personality, and a history.

In discussing the examination of human remains from that war, team member Nick Saunders examined the period from 1919 to 1990 and stated that:

Some individuals during this time (and still today) specialised in locating human remains and stripping them of their military equipment and personal belongings – German helmets, firearms, uniforms, regimental badges and insignia were especially sought, and became increasingly valuable over time. By virtue of the clandestine nature of this activity, the authorities were usually not informed, and the human remains themselves were quickly and unceremoniously reburied.[13]

ABOVE *One of the many graves of the 33rd Battalion, AIF, in Toronto Avenue cemetery, Ploegsteert Wood. Note the Australian flag placed in front of the grave.*

The man that was discovered by our excavations at St Yvon had not been looted, which is important for the potential of obtaining an identity for the individual. This situation was certainly helped when the John Laffin wrote that 'AIF battlefields which are less likely to be fruitful include Messines. ...The AIF was moving rapidly at this time; battles were concluded in a matter of hours and the Diggers were never in one place for long.'[14] Although Laffin believed his work encouraged battlefield 'archaeology', his methodologies could prove damaging to systematic approaches to forensic examinations of sites at a later stage; his belief that Messines would not reveal many relics of the Australian role in the war was fortunate.

Following the recovery of the body, official attempts at identification began, conducted in Belgium at the behest of the Commonwealth War Graves Commission and Australian government. Naturally enough, the first stage would be to examine the identity disc. If this were to prove unsuccessful, then the Army Historian in Canberra would try to inspect all documentation that might indicate which unit the soldier might have belonged to, in conjunction with an examination of the remains of the man and his associated artefacts. In addition, brigade and battalion diaries are useful resources, alongside the records of the Australian Red Cross Society and others.

Terror and Trophies

From the strands of evidence available to the authors, we could also try to build up a picture of the man whose remains we had found. Firstly, in an endeavour to gain an identity for him and, secondly, to try to provide some information about the man himself, his personality, his character. When writing on the role of forensic archaeological attempts to recover missing US service persons from the Vietnam War, Swift wrote: 'The value of an artefact lies not so much in its age or its beauty as in the information it provides about the people who produced it and the uses to which it was put. Its proximity to other relics, to features of terrain – its entire context – tells a scientist much about the article and its place

in the past'. The job of the forensic specialist on the battlefield is to solve 'personal riddles – identifying the dead, establishing cause of death, finding clues to the circumstances surrounding a life's end.'[15]

Given where he was found, what he was wearing, and what he carried, we feel there is a strong probability that he was from one of the earlier companies of the 33rd Battalion, 9th Brigade, Australian 3rd Division, killed in the attacks of the Battle of Messines. He was, after all, found right in the centre of the attacking positions of this unit for the 1917 action. We know that he was killed in 1916 or afterwards as he was wearing the Brodie helmet and carried a box respirator, both of which were introduced in 1916. Furthermore, his wallet held 1916-dated French coins. The main Australian presence here occurred in 1917 at Messines and, although Australian units were here later in the war, this was largely artillery. The soldier we found was not in winter clothing so perhaps the June 1917 action is most likely. In later waves of the Battle of Messines, the Australian 4th Division pushed to secondary objectives, but this was through the New Zealanders to the north, towards Messines itself. A member of the 33rd Battalion in the actions of 7 June 1917 seems the most probable.

There are further details that as archaeologists we were able to obtain from the physical remains, evidence gained both on the excavation site and also in the conservations laboratory. We know that this soldier had just had a haircut as Rob Janaway found clippings of hair around the remnants of the collar of his uniform around the 'rising sun' badges. Perhaps not surprisingly he also had lice, with these being visible under microscopic analysis.

What can one then discern about the man from the finds with him? He seemed to have had a great fear of gas, understandable if he had been a member of the 33rd Battalion, as these soldiers, along with many others in the assaulting units of the 3rd Division, had taken many casualties of gas inhalation as they had approached the stopping-off trenches through Ploegsteert Wood.

Cyril Herborn of the 33rd Battalion AIF, one of twelve men attached to B Company HQ as a

signaller and runner, recounted the experience of the gas attack:

> *It was last Wednesday night about 9. We left our billets at Nieppe for the trenches at Ploegsteert. It was about four miles, but it seemed more, and just as we entered the wood, about a mile or so before we reached the line, we had to don our gas masks. Fritz had sent gas over. It was pitch dark and we had a 'contact' picking our way along the duckboards with our helmets on. They are bad enough if you just lie down in them, but much worse in the circumstances of that night. Two of our chaps were gassed. Poor old Dick Holtsbaum was one, up to the time of leaving the other day I could not find what really happened to him, but some say he died. I hope it is not true.*[16]

Go to Toronto Avenue Cemetery today and the results of this German defensive tactic are visible.

Our soldier had rubber-backed gas goggles, a PH hood, and small box respirator. Although worn at the alert, his respirator was not actually on. He also had a degree of field experience; he had added two rounds into his rifle strap to stop the adjuster slipping, and had also removed one shoulder title to place in his back pocket. This is perhaps something he was unlikely to have gleaned at the Bustard, although it is possible that the nursery sector near Armentières gave him this.

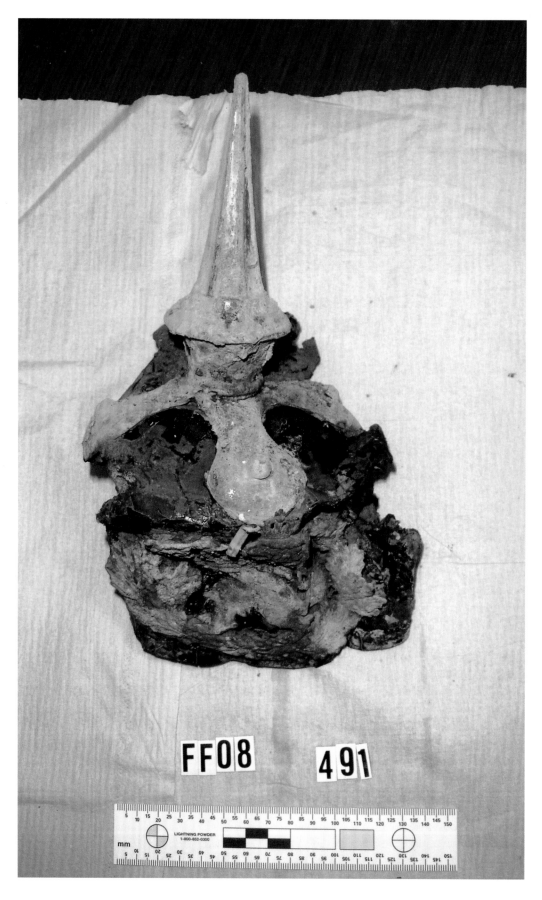

RIGHT *One of the sensational finds made with the Australian was the* Pickelhaube *in his backpack. Items such as this were much prized as souvenirs and help to tell a story about the soldier.*

The most striking element of finds associated with the body was that he had a souvenir in his pack – the pickelhaube. This was the top souvenir available to the Allied soldier of the First World War. An object of patent leather with fluted silver spike and bearing the crest of Hesse – a crowned lion rampant holding a sword – even among other helmets of the type, this one would have looked both unusual and impressive. It was certainly not something that the soldier would have left behind in his kit bag to be taken by men in the reserve areas. Cyril Herborn of the 33rd Battalion was certainly one of those members of the AIF who found the aftermath of Messines to be rich for souvenirs:

Sunday morning [10 June] was very favourable for searching round for souvenirs – it being very misty. There were lots of dead Fritzs about and worst of all some of ours too. But most of the Fritzs had been robbed of any souvenirs they had. There were whips [lots] of material lying about, machine-gun belts galore at one place, and plenty of German rifles. There were German packs, equipment and ration bags. Most of us already had good souvenirs. I had a new looking officer's cap, but someone pinched it from my heap of belongings while I was away.[17]

Perhaps this fear of one's mates stealing prized souvenirs was the reason our man had his pickelhaube in his pack even on the battlefield.

Many of the bronze chinstrap segments of this helmet were also present and it was found alongside buckles of packs and food tins that one would more commonly expect to see. The Hessian regiments were not present in the St Yvon sector and so, in addition to the stratigraphic evidence, is added proof that this was not an item thrown from the trench by its German owner as and when it became outmoded through the introduction of the M1916 helmet. Furthermore, the condition of the pickelhaube some 90 years on was such that it would also have been unlikely that its owner would have thrown it away as damaged. The pickelhaube was a souvenir or relic of war that was recognisable the world over. One in

the Pitt-Rivers Museum in Oxford even made it back to the Naga Hills in north-east India where, now adorned with a pair of horns, it probably represented a 'symbolic substitute of a captured enemy head trophy and proof of valour in battle';[18] it was taken by one of the Naga Labour Corps that had fought with the British forces.

Thus our Australian was someone who took souvenirs. 'The First World War was, as many soldiers observed at the time, a "war of souvenirs". So common was the hunt for souvenirs that the term "souveniering" became a thinly veiled euphemism for looting.'[19] Having been captured at the Battle of Messines, Hans Ludwig, 6th Company, Reserve Infantry Regiment 120, encountered a number of English soldiers: 'They were darned nice, but they were souvenir hounds like the rest of the Englishmen and took all the buttons off my uniform. I had a helluva job convincing an Englishman that a pair of eye glasses, which I had in my pocket, was hardly a souvenir to be proud of, especially as I needed them so badly.' The most famous doyen of this art was himself an Australian, admittedly originally hailing from Liverpool: John 'Barney' Hines of the 45th Battalion. One, probably apocryphal, story even suggested that the Kaiser saw images of Hines with his trophies and put a bounty on the head of this 'barbarian'.

The collecting of relics was therefore not unusual – a pickelhaube in this condition, however, would have been a prize asset and one which the soldier we found had been keen to keep hold of even if it encumbered him as he went into action.

So much then for the context of burial, equipment and possessions leading to a narrative of events on the soldier's role in action and his personality. Who was he? Unfortunately, his identity disc was far too degraded for the University of Ghent to be able to gain any information from it. There are, however, many possibilities that could lead to an identification of the man. For example, there might be visible service numbers on his spoon (through the use of x-rays), or the chance of gaining serial numbers on the steel disc of the rifle butt to reveal the unit in which he served.

ABOVE *'Souvenir King' 2296 Private John 'Barney' Hines, A Company, 45th Battalion, with his trophies (souvenirs) obtained on the morning of the advance of the 4th and 13th Brigades at Polygon Wood, in the Ypres Sector, during the Third Battle of Ypres. This photograph was taken by Frank Hurley on 27 September 1917. AWM E00822*

Much of the work of archaeologists, including drawing together information towards identification, must be circumstantial, but can be correlated to provide a convincing, overall picture. To an extent the maxim of Sherlock Holmes in *The Sign of Four* rings true: 'Eliminate all other factors, and the one which remains must be the truth.'[20] From this position, one can then apply other scientific techniques.

This is where one has to examine the body itself, and a forensic anthropological examination of the remains would give an approximate height and age of the man, while also showing any earlier trauma or physical attributes – perhaps even as to whether he was left- or right-handed. This would clearly narrow down the search when compared against the documentary lists of the missing. Dental pathology could also prove useful, particularly as the Australians have at least partial records for their soldiers. There are still further scientific techniques that could be used to examine the clippings of hair to establish hair colour – this is necessary to examine melanin content and to ensure there has been no post-depositional change in colour. Most of

An informal group portrait of unidentified Australian soldiers sporting helmets (Pickelhauben) and caps captured from the Germans in the battle of Pozières. Some have their hands raised, possibly in a feigned gesture of surrender. In the front on the ground is a Lewis gun. July 1916. AWM EZ0135

the prehistoric bog bodies found in Europe, for example, have red hair as a result of their lying in acidic, peaty water for over a millennium, rather than being a true reflection of original hair colour.

After this work, forensic science could utilise isotope and/or strontium analysis of the enamel of the man's teeth, as this could indicate where he grew up. This technique cannot locate the precise village of origin but can provide a broad indication of region. It could, at least, say whether he grew up in England or Australia and this is significant given that two of the missing 33rd Battalion soldiers were from Sheffield (Yorkshire) and Chelmsford (Essex).

The final factor would be to examine the DNA of the individual, as was done with the five soldiers from Zonnebeke – with three identities being gained through this technique. For this to work, it is only really practical to start with a small set of possibilities, having used all the above elements beforehand and having considered all the information of archaeological context. One also needs a database of DNA matches to check against, from surviving relatives. It is interesting to note that, utterly unprompted, a number of relatives of the missing from the Battle of Messines have come forwards to this end.

Following the removal of the remains of the man and their retrieval by the Belgian Army on behalf of the Commonwealth War Graves Commission, the excavation team paid their own commemoration to the man on site in a small ceremony and later visited the Ploegsteert Memorial where we laid a wreath to commemorate the fallen. James, a piper with our group, piped both the 'Last Post' and 'Waltzing Matilda' in recognition of the occasion. The Australians, too, had their pipe band, one which had even paraded through Market Lavington during the Australian training period on Salisbury Plain.

Excavating a site of this nature, admittedly, is not like working with prehistoric or Roman remains; this man might have a surviving spouse, sibling, or child. Such facts add a huge extra level of poignancy, of requirements for due dignity of treatment of remains, of restrictions, of reward. As a member of the Australian 3rd Division, this man might have stood in Martin's (co-author of this work) home village in Wiltshire some 90 years before, or might have seen co-author Richard's grandfather, something the author himself never did. The immediacy of First World War archaeology is at times astonishing. For all the sepia-toned and monochrome images of this war, the archaeology team had found so much that had colour to it.

Over 60,000 Australian soldiers were killed in the First World War. Of these, 6,000 died in Belgium and have no known grave. These men are all commemorated on the Menin Gate. We hope that all the information recovered by the team will lead to the identification of the soldier we found and that, eventually, the Menin Gate will hold one less name. Nevertheless, if this is not achieved, he will still have been reburied with dignity and commemoration for the first time, and the evidence he carried with him in death will at least have ensured that part of the man's story and character survived. In a poem written in 1918 about the Battle of Messines, a soldier of the Australian 3rd Division wrote: 'Strange sights are seen upon that battleground, but stranger still are unearthed from below.'[21] He was right.

[1] Spagnoly and Smith, 2003: 98.
[2] Roelens and Bril, 2006 (b).
[3] Roelens and Bril, 2006 (a): 265.
[4] Roelens and Bril, Ibid.: 265.
[5] Lynch, 2008: 188.
[6] <http://www.awm.gov.au/cms_images/AWM4/23/AWM4-23-50-8.pdf> AWM4 Australian Imperial Force Unit War Diaries, 1914–18 War, Infantry, Item No 23/50/8, 33rd Infantry Battalion, June 1917).
[7] <http://www.awm.gov.au/cms_images/AWM4/23/AWM4-23-9-8.pdf> Australian Imperial Force Unit War Diaries, 1914–18 War, Infantry, Item No 23/9/8, 9th Infantry Brigade, June 1917.
[8] Ibid.
[9] Bostyn et al., 2007: 224.
[10] Ibid., 227.
[11] Anon, 1920: 3.
[12] Bostyn et al., Ibid.: 231, 234.
[13] Saunders, 2007:10.
[14] Laffin, 1993: 40.
[15] Swift, 2003: 36–7.
[16] Edwards, 1996: 42. NB Dick Holtsbaum recovered from the gas attack but died of wounds in a later battle, on 4 October 1917, being buried at Lijssenthoek cemetery.
[17] Edwards, Ibid.: 44.
[18] Saunders, 2003: 183.
[19] Saunders, 2007: 35.
[20] Conan Doyle, 1993: 114.
[21] Cuttriss, 1918: 92 – Messines.

OPPOSITE *On the first Friday of every month a memorial service takes place at the Ploegsteert Memorial. Here, on the last day of the excavation in 2007, Lt-Col Paul Smith of the Australian Army lays a wreath of commemoration on behalf of the Australian government.*

CHAPTER 10

CSI Flanders

As we have seen, there are numerous pressures surrounding the excavation of human remains. The various legal authorities need to be kept updated and work can only proceed at *their* pace, rather than that of the excavators. However, the methodology can be established at the outset to achieve the objectives, which include:

Recovery of the body

▨ *The creation of written, drawn and photographic archaeological records, which will assist in identification and interpretation of remains.*

▨ *Artefactual and dating information that can inform the historical research and may lead to various levels of identification.*

OPPOSITE *Essential to any fieldwork is immediate conservation of finds. Dr Rob Janaway of Bradford University is a core member of the excavation team and has evaluated innovative methods of conservation for 20th century materials. Here he looks at one of the Australian collar dogs.*

LEFT *Under the watchful eyes of both Belgian police and army, the excavation forensics team work with the the body of the Australian soldier.*

■ *Evidence-led interpretation of remains – which comes later but should be discussed and tested on site.*

In order to achieve this, the highest archaeological standards must be maintained on site and may borrow techniques from forensic archaeology. To this end the following steps were taken:

■ *The site was secured and taped off to prevent unnecessary access and disturbance to the team.*

■ *Volunteers acted as overnight security to prevent unwanted visitors.*

■ *A tent was secured from Commonwealth War Graves so that work could continue in bad weather.*

■ *The exhumation team was selected and given designated roles within the operation: Team leader – a senior forensic archaeologist.*
Two archaeologists, one of whom is also a physical anthropologist.
Conservator, to advise on the lifting of, and care for, artefacts.
Site planner, to create a drawn record.
Two site recorders, one to create an inventory of objects recovered, the other to maintain a running narrative of times and events, including visitors, lifting of objects and pertinent comments made by team members.
Photographer, taking fixed-point images to record process, and detailed, in-situ images of significant evidence.
EOD [Explosive Ordnance Disposal?] cover.

In addition we also had an in-house video team who recorded much of the work.

Once work commenced, every object recovered was given an individual 'Special Find' number and packaged separately. Their discovery position was marked onto the site plan and photographs were taken. The exception to this was a live Mills No 5 hand grenade! Objects were then returned to the temporary laboratory at the accommodation for stabilisation and basic

RIGHT *A pickle jar recovered from an excavation trench. Like HP Sauce, pickles added a little variety to soldiers' otherwise bland diet.*

LEFT *Forensic archaeologists Brian Shottenkirk and Steve Litherland work to complete recovery of the body.*

cleaning, prior to packaging and transfer to the authorities. The conservation side proved invaluable in retrieving information, as the chapter on the body makes clear.

The exhumation followed a similar method, with identifiable groups of bones being bagged together, such as right hand, or left foot. The articulated vertebrae were lifted in a block and wrapped in silver foil to maintain their integrity.

Once all human remains and associated artefacts were believed to be clear from the area there was further cleaning and inspection of the ground, as well as limited metal detector survey, to ensure nothing had been missed. Then a final record of the context in which the body had been found was made, including the normal archaeological processes of section drawings and a post-excavation plan.

Practicalities

A number of practical issues had to be negotiated. First, the entire team wanted to be kept informed and, if possible, to see, if not participate. This involved balancing these legitimate aspirations against the need for the team to work unhindered. Fortunately, breaks provided the perfect opportunity for this.

Breaks are essential. Although the team was totally focused on the job, lack of refreshment and proper breaks could lead to low blood sugar, friction and 'tunnel vision', so it was important to ensure that food and drink were available when required, even at 10pm on the evening of the discovery, and that people took time out.

External visitors became an issue. Once word had got out that there was a body, local people wished to see and the landowner wanted to bring his family. This is part of a diplomatic exercise that is properly undertaken, but again it was useful to have the site French-speakers on alert to assist in managing visitors and generally to ensure that work could proceed unimpeded.

The team had to be told that there was a total embargo on news of the discovery and that pictures of the skeleton were not to appear on the web. This was at the request of the Australians, who, rightly, didn't want potential relatives to see a body in so public a forum. In addition, news management reduced the chance for nocturnal visitors.

Most importantly, the local frameworks and legislation had to be observed. It was essential that the landowner was kept informed but he was only the first among many interested parties. In the first instance, the discovery of

any body must be reported to the police, for obvious reasons. Once they have visited and ascertained that it is of First World War vintage they will inform the King's Procurator, whose role includes that of coroner, who has the final say on the nature of the burial. He will hand responsibility for the removal and safe storage of remains over to the Belgian Army, who take care of the remains and any associated artefacts until they are passed to the Commonwealth War Graves Commission. CWGC are also informed, as a courtesy, both locally and through contacts at their headquarters.

While this diplomacy was time-consuming and mostly carried out in French, as the local language, it was utterly essential that proper procedures were followed. The detailed recording of on-site activity and inventories of finds were also regarded as part of this process, so that appropriate behaviour was not only followed but documented. As a result the local authorities were both clear and happy that the No Man's Land team is a competent body where human remains of the conflict are concerned.

The Missing Soldiers of the First World War – Jon Price

The No Man's Land archaeological team have excavated the remains of a number of the 'missing' from excavations on First World War sites, British, Australian, and German. We have seen the way the team dealt with the discovery of the Australian soldier at St Yvon, but there are, of course, thousands of others who are still categorised as 'missing'. Jon Price, one of the pioneers of First World War archaeology, examines the wider phenomenon of this group:

The First World War was the first conflict in which the use of modern weaponry and munitions on an industrial scale, in generally static warfare, produced massive numbers of casualties. The British Imperial forces suffered 832,680 killed, the Germans 1,600,000, of which 364,625 British and Imperial soldiers, and 103,000 German soldiers were listed as missing. The other combatant nations suffered

RIGHT *The bodies of Australian troops who were killed during the final battles on the Western Front are gathered for burial at a cemetery under construction at Guillemont Farm, 3 October 1918.* IWM E (AUS) 4945

similar losses. An indication of the scale of the problem for the combatants is the fact that there are no completely accurate figures available. These casualties were not all suffered on the Western Front, as the war was also fought in eastern Europe, the Middle East and Africa; however, the Western Front was the place where the greatest numbers of casualties were caused in the most continuous way from 1914 to 1918.

It might be thought that soldiers were mostly missing because the sheer destructive power of the weaponry destroyed their physical remains, and it is the case that where excavation has been carried out at sites where mine warfare took place (Auchy-les-Mines, Ploegsteert) detached body parts and bone fragments have been recovered. In fact, it is becoming clear that many of the missing were buried on the battlefield, or at medical posts, but that their grave sites were subsequently lost, and that some battle casualties were never recovered as a result of accidental burial by shell bursts (Serre, Ploegsteert), or through trench or dugout collapse.

The bodies of these missing soldiers are still regularly recovered as a result of accidental finds during development, or through ploughing, and increasingly on officially sanctioned archaeological excavations. From these controlled excavations it is possible to build up a picture of how the soldiers on both sides dealt with their dead, and with the dead of their opponents, on the battlefield.

From excavations carried out by the No Man's Land team on the Somme at Serre, on the Ypres salient at Bikschote, and on the Loos battlefield at Auchy-les-Mines, it appears that during battles the Germans buried soldiers within 2 to 5m of their own trenches. Often these burials, though carried out carefully, made use of shell-holes (Serre, Auchy), but on at least some occasions (Auchy) standard-sized shallow grave cuts have been recognised. There is also evidence of post-battle clearance, where several bodies have been found in the same grave, sometimes buried with care, sometimes clearly thrown in without ceremony (Auchy, Bikschote).

The recovery and burial of the dead was initially the responsibility of their unit at the front line, or of the medical teams at forward casualty clearing stations and field hospitals. During and after the war military battlefield clearance teams were responsible for the recovery and identification of bodies, with graves registration units keeping the record of the grave locations and the individual soldiers they contained. The identification of recovered soldiers remains a military matter, and in Belgium this work is overseen by the Belgian military.

The Imperial War Graves Commission was established by the British government in 1917 to set up and manage the cemeteries, and their work is continued by the Commonwealth War Graves Commission (CWGC). The German *Volksbund Deutsche Kriegsgräberfürsorge* (VDK), set up in 1919, has always been a non-governmental organisation, but it has the same role of setting up and managing cemeteries. In both cases the cemeteries contain memorials listing missing soldiers, and graves containing unknown soldiers. In the case of the CWGC these are marked as 'a soldier known only to God', and in the case of the VDK an '*Unbekannt Soldat*' (unknown soldier). Often a nationality is added, sometimes a regiment, and occasionally a rank, where these facts are known.

The identification of the recovered soldiers is the chief goal, and the biggest problem, when they are found. German soldiers were issued with an aluminium identity tag, and where soil conditions are suitable these can survive. British and Imperial troops had identity tags made of compressed fibre; these are extremely unlikely to survive.

Many soldiers, like the Australian from St Yvon, carried specially made identity tags or bracelets. Sometimes watches (Forward Cottage), or jewellery are found with names engraved, and even items of kit such as spoons

can be inscribed with names or numbers. Occasionally more fragile materials survive; in rare instances these can include letters and pay books (Auchy-les-Mines).

Even where identification is missing it is sometimes possible, by comparing dating evidence with unit histories and lists of casualties to narrow down the probable identity of the soldier. This would once have been the end of the trail, but it is now possible to compare the DNA of recovered soldiers with that of their likely descendants, or as we have seen, to examine other elements such as the strontium levels in the teeth. This procedure has a financial cost, and the VDK is unable to provide funds for this. The British MOD, although in principle willing to carry out this investigation, almost never considers it to be cost-effective. As mentioned, the Australian MOD has, however, used DNA investigation to identify several recovered soldiers.

British Commonwealth, and German recovered soldiers, whether identified or not, are buried in cemeteries close to where they were killed. For the British and Commonwealth soldiers a military ceremony is arranged, and surviving direct relatives are brought to the ceremony at the government's expense. German soldiers are buried with a civilian ceremony, and no assistance is available for the attendance of relatives.

LEFT *Three dead German soldiers lie in the wreckage of their shelter after the Battle of Pilckem Ridge, 31 July 1917.* IWM Q3117

CHAPTER 11

Emotional Landscapes

The Western Front affects different people in different ways. While those with ancestral connections to the sites may be expected to react to the landscape in an immediate way, the scale of events, numbers, trauma and loss evokes a multiplicity of responses from visitors. The same is true of the excavation team. Like any archaeological landscape, the study area is multi-vocal, a term used to express the numerous ideas, theories and responses that come from the landscape and its history.

Any archaeological fieldwork, whether field survey or excavation, will engender engagement among participants; this comes from spending time looking at, walking in, and working on, a piece of ground and becoming intimately enmeshed in it. Archaeologists may be seen as performers within the landscape, enacting a drama that both reveals and expresses the hidden history of the landscape and the individuals within it. As such it is a deeply human, collaborative and emotional experience. However, some schools of archaeological thought insist that archaeology is a scientific discipline, that practitioners should remain detached, dispassionate and objective. But the experience of archaeologists working in the period of the First World War is that it remains an emotionally fraught exercise. In the first instance the scientific approach to archaeology fails to recognise the attachments that individuals and teams make with their

OPPOSITE *The team record the British trenches and trench boards at St Yvon. From left to right: Justin Russell, Gontrand Callewaert, Steve Litherland, Dan Phillips.*

BELOW *A patrol prepares to raid the German trenches. Moments after this photograph was taken a shell killed and injured several of these men.* IWM Q5098

ABOVE *A now-peaceful view across no-man's-land to Ultimo crater from the British lines.*

subjects, while in the second the proximity and traumatic nature of events under study on the Western Front engender emotional responses from the investigators. On some sites this experience has been deepened by external factors, such as the identification of bodies recovered and subsequent contacts with their families, or by the resonances that particular sites may have through family connection or a wider cultural landscape, such as trenches associated with doomed poet Wilfred Owen.

In addition, external pressure may be felt where there is a possibility of identifying sets of remains. Even more so than on sites of other periods, skeletons of this war are more than simply data. The fact that wider society refers to them as 'The Missing', or 'The Glorious Dead', is not to be dismissed lightly, nor is to stand at the Ploegsteert Memorial and wonder about those 'missing' who may yet be encountered in excavations.

The emotional issues were reinforced for the team in 2007 when a number of them assisted in the commemoration of the 90th anniversary of the Battle of Passchendale. Re-enactors were

due to start a memorial march at 03:30 on 31 July, 90 years to the minute of Zero Hour. The team were asked to provide volunteers to fire flares along the line of march as the re-enactors set out. Everyone involved commented on the darkness and the eerie sensation of seeing flares light the sky, of hearing boots on the road and seeing the figures emerging from the darkness; figures all but identical to the men whose story they were researching.

Kin Groups and Comrades

The First World War affected countries, communities and families. By 1918 almost everyone in the combatant nations had been touched by the war. In the same way, many of the archaeological team have connections with the war. A poll of members revealed that most know of an ancestor who was in uniform during the conflict; some of our American colleagues had ancestors on both sides of

the lines, reflecting the fact that much of the population of the US comprises European immigrants. One American member tells of family meals ending in heated argument and even violence because each side had family members fighting for opposing nations. Another, relates the damage done to her family because of the death of her great-grandfather, whose loss reduced the family to poverty. Yet another talks of an Irish ancestor's service in British uniform, an interesting association because for many years the Republic had a semi-official silence in respect of those who served the Empire. The authors themselves are no exception: Richard's grandfather was with the Australian artillery train supporting the assault, while Martin's grandfather, an Ulsterman, was serving with 99th Field Ambulance, part of the Royal Army Medical Corps, and was en route toward a hospital on the River Somme, having been relieved from the La Fontaine sector. He would shortly be handling casualties from the Passchendale offensive.

Several other team members are either serving or former British military, including Army and Royal Air Force. They understand the experiences and service of the First World War soldiers by virtue of the fact that they have worn uniform, trained and endured hardship. This engagement is a personal embodiment of Army ethos that is instilled in troops at all levels through ritual, ceremony, battlefield tours and military history. It is the same process as that manifested in the New Zealanders' model at Cannock Chase; the soldiers of yesteryear may be said to still be leading by example. The experience of the modern soldier can afford insights into the events of 90 years ago, as the Tabasco anecdote illustrates.

Meanwhile, others in uniform visited the site, such as the participants in the memorial march, giving the team the chance to see First World War equipment of both sides close up. As one of the British re-enactors was carrying blank ammunition, the team also got to see and hear a Lee Enfield rifle firing. Some of the re-enactors were much the same age as the soldiers who fought, and the team found it unnerving to see their subjects walking, and in colour, adding a soundtrack to the normally quiet practice of archaeology.

ABOVE *A group of archaeologists and those that took part in the march to commemorate the 90th anniversary of Passchendaele discuss some of the archaeological findings.*

The Name on the Wall

One team member has a particular engagement with the site. Tori tells her story here:

The Plugstreet Project has extremely well-defined research questions; the answers to some of these are contained within this volume, with others to follow as the excavation continues. Like many periods, reconstruction is not done solely through archaeology, but is reinforced with historical documentation, some of which helps to provide the research questions. The archaeologist will also find much more personal and graphic representation of this period through film and photographic images, entries in diaries, journals, and, most poignantly, personal letters.

BELOW *A panel on the Ploegsteert memorial with the name of Tori's great uncle.*

Furthermore many will have personally known someone who lived through those times and whose recollections can provide very tangible links with the conflict.

For me, such a person was my grandmother who, as a girl in London during the Great War, experienced it on the 'home front'. Details of the death of her brother, Stan, in the trenches very early in the Great War were consigned to the small 'black box' that is our family archive. A few years ago my father sorted out the contents so that he could construct a family tree, principally for the benefit of my sisters, brother and myself. In the process he was only able to muster two postcards, a very short letter and a photo that concerned Stan. These artefacts, together with a couple of letters of condolence were the sum total of what we then knew about him.

The photo (taken in a Dover studio) shows a very young and raw soldier, preparing to face the unknown. It is a photo of Stan just before his embarkation. In a postcard posted in Southampton the day he was embarking for Europe, he describes to his parents how up-beat and happy everyone seemed as they were played aboard. Then there is a short letter from the trenches, not only his first but, alas, his last (he was killed just 20 days later). In it he describes with stark clarity what was going on all around him. Nevertheless he concludes on an optimistic note that is astonishingly mature for a lad still in his teens. Finally, there is a postcard written to Stan's mother from her brother enquiring after Stan's fate, after hearing that he had been injured, and that he would make further enquiries from a friend of his who was due to return from the trenches shortly.

It transpired that Stan was never to return from the trenches. To these documents, my father added a citation from the CWGC website indicating that Stan was killed on 31 October 1914 and has no known grave, but that his name appears on Plate 5 of the Ploegsteert Memorial.

This last piece of information was uncovered just as I had been accepted onto the Ploegsteert excavation, and is one of many coincidences that have drawn me to towards Stan.

So I left for Ploegsteert equipped with not just my trowel, but carrying this information about Stan and the hope that I might be able to take a good photo of his entry on the memorial. Partly because of this connection, I was one of those chosen to represent the NML team by laying the wreath during the Last Post ceremony due to take place on the last day of the excavation.

With the help of Ralph Whitehead who was one my allies in the German bunker trench excavation, we duly laid the wreath. Members of Ralph's family had fought on the German side during the war and so it proved fitting to lay the team's wreath together. I had thought I might cope well with seeing Stan's name, together with hundreds of others, at close range – especially as I had begun to appreciate the conditions in which these men had lived and died, and the sheer scale of the human suffering involved – but I found it far harder than I had expected. Yet I wanted to discover more about what happened to Stan.

Luckily for me, the No Man's Land team's combined knowledge and their enthusiasm meant that it was not long before I was handed a profile on Stan and his military record. I now know that he died along with eight other men of his battalion that day during a battle near the Messines Road. This means that he was probably killed just metres away from the trench I had been excavating, and that on the many occasions that I took a short rest from the concrete and looked up over the trench across the fields to the church at Messines, I was looking out over the land where his remains may still be. It is saddening to think of the men described by Stan in his only letter from Belgium, as lying dead just in front of his trench and know in only days the same fate awaited him.

I am asked how I would feel about returning to these fields to excavate, knowing that Stan's remains may be lying out there. I truly cannot think of a better way to commemorate Stan and his fellow soldiers than to be part of a professional and respectful team dedicated to furthering our knowledge of this conflict and in so doing remembering those who were part of it. The practical archaeologist and realist in me knows that the chances of his remains being recovered are extremely small, but whatever led me to a field in Belgium where my great-uncle died over 90 years ago, be that coincidence or fate, demonstrates that our individual stories can continue long after death. Surely archaeology is all about these stories, and perhaps Stan's is not yet over. ...

The Epitome of War

The epitome of war, commented US General S.L.A. Marshall, is the battlefield. The battlefield is where armies are made and destroyed but beneath these words is an uncomfortable truth – that the battlefield is a place of death. Everyone on the team is aware of this but the reality, the face of battle, emerging from the ground in the shape of human remains is another matter entirely.

Following the discovery and recovery of the Australian body in 2008, team anthropologist Dr Paola Filipucci conducted interviews with some of the members. While some address the issue of the body, others consider the wider experience of involvement in the excavation.

Avril – archaeologist

Although she is an archaeologist, Avril has never excavated a body. She is not directly involved in excavating the body at Plugstreet. Avril doesn't have any relatives that she knows of involved in the war. For her, what is most poignant about the war is the number of dead, as seen graphically on the monuments – the sheer number of names for instance on the Thiepval memorial. Seeing the individual body is somewhat less poignant, although likes the idea of potentially 'taking one name off the list' of the missing if the body is identified. She also feels the importance of being able to give him a proper burial instead of 'leaving him in a field to be ploughed up'. She has seen the body first when only the boots were visible, then when the whole was exposed, but the different exposure hasn't made a difference for her. She doesn't feel, however, that it would be proper to take photos, probably because she would be showing them to other people and that would feel like voyeurism. It is OK to take shots for the archaeological record but she wouldn't like to see the photos on the web as part of someone's holiday snaps.

Egg – photographer

Her first time on an archaeological dig, Egg has a long-term interest in the First World War, developed as a child, perhaps because at primary school the teacher always observed the two-minute silence on Remembrance Day and even then she found it moving. Egg saw the body first when the feet were exposed, then the whole body. She wanted to see it.

She felt emotional and tearful afterwards. It made her think of how the soldier at the time might have been afraid of dying in a field, in a foreign place. She feels that it is better to be at rest in a cemetery than in a battlefield – a place of battle and violence (no 'rest' there). Egg has read a lot on the First World War, fiction initially, then some history books and diaries, and eventually her great-great-uncles' letters. She did so because she wanted to learn something more intimate than what you read in books. She found that she was thinking about the dead soldier today while walking around in the fields near the dig.

Kat – archaeology student

Kat has a family connection with the First World War but found also she had developed an interest which led her to want to come

BELOW *Now covered in moss, this is one of the numerous surviving bunkers still present in Ploegsteert Wood.*

to this dig. 'For some reason I get emotional about WWI, not like crying, but I feel something'. She is one of the team members who volunteer to spend part of the night guarding the remains. She explains that she 'really wanted to see this place at night'. At first there were the combine harvesters disturbing the night, but eventually 'when it was quiet we saw the flashes of lightning and we started talking about how it was the same as in the war, only without the noise'. It was then that her companion told her about the football match and how it had taken place nearby: 'It was that which brought it home to me, the reality of it.' Kat then tells of visiting Verdun and Belleau Wood with her family, as a child. 'Verdun was a quiet town; as a child I felt like I was in a giant church, there were only tourists and they went around as if it was sacred.' As for Belleau Wood, 'I don't remember hearing any birds. ... So that's why I wanted to experience it [Plugstreet Wood] in the quiet.' At no point in the interview does she mentions the soldier in particular: her focus seems to be on the place and landscape and the soldiers' experience.

Glen – countryside manager

He has an interest in the First World War though not a 'passion'. It is his first time on an archaeological excavation but he has dug before, working in countryside management and the building trade. He has an interest in architecture and also in archaeology and the past. He recalls a long time ago while working on a building site coming across remains of a medieval building and while the other builders just dug through it, 'I couldn't help digging it carefully, I found myself working like an archaeologist, really slowly looking for clues' because it's the past, which we need to conserve and respect and not destroy. He found it 'fascinating' to find bodies, and says he has always been interested in ancient remains of the dead: even as a child he was always fascinated by 'life and death'. As for the soldier, he saw the boots first, and took a picture of them; then saw him again much later on, when the remains had all been exposed. He can understand why we might want to rebury him, to give him a proper burial, but

sometimes with archaeology as a whole 'I have a feeling that says "leave it there" ...We are just another civilisation passing through, there will be other civilisations after us', and it seems somehow wrong 'that we are digging stuff up just in the name of our own knowledge. Some of the story should be left for others.' Glen speaks again about the soldier, how 'he had everything with him'; he found this 'a poignant reminder of the reality of the situation', making being in touch with the past event more tangible, especially as he was still wearing recognisable kit. More generally, finding the body was a sort of 'icing on the cake for the dig', part of the dig 'taking form', and the outcome of all the activity which initially seems rather unformed, unfocused. 'The Great War is getting historical but it's still close. I grew up with two world wars behind me (obviously, I didn't live through them); for instance my grandfather was born in 1898, he was in the Great War – he was in England servicing vehicles [as an engineer]. ... When I think that he joined in 1916 voluntarily (to avoid conscription and so to ensure a greater choice of where he was placed – which possibly enabled him to survive the war) and that he might have met "Charlie" [the dead soldier] in the street. Further still, had Charlie survived, I could have met him in the street, because he was about my Grandfather's age. ... You learn about the past from books and museums but with archaeology you find something very very real, you can't deny that sort of thing.'

Jo – conservation manager

This is Jo's second year at Plugstreet. She has a family link with the First World War. She says she was 'fascinated' about finding the body: 'I was there when they found the boots – when Graham said there is definitely leg bone inside and stood back several paces.' It wasn't the long bones but the hand that struck her most: the hand seemed 'very intimate'. She recalls sifting through silt to find any tiny finger bones, found two and later borrowed a bone manual 'to work it all out'. The hand was intact and 'made him into a person' because 'it was over his head, as if protecting his head'. When asked if he should be excavated she says yes, because he is one of the missing 'who is no

LIAN INF.
RIVATE

33RD BN. AUSTRALIAN INF.

PRIVATE	PRIVATE
CRAGG W.	MAHER W. J.
DELANEY W. C. M.M.	MARZAN W.
DONOGHUE C. T.	MATCHETT V. C.
DOUST H. E. C.	MATHER A. J.
EVANS G. E.	MILLINGTON J.
FLETCHER T. J.	MILROY J. T.
GERARD W.	MOONEY P. T.
GILL W. T.	MURPHY W. E.
GORDON J. A.	NERLICH O. B.
GUEST W.	NILSSON N.
HALL C. D.	ORMAN D. G.
HARRIS C. A.	PAGE J. J. I.
HAY J. A.	PARKIN J.
HEATH E.	PASCOE L. J.
HEYWOOD S. J.	PEACOCK F.
HOLLOWAY A. N.	PEARCE O. G.
HOLLOWAY T. W.	POMFRET W.
HYDE T. E.	PRINGLE R. N.
KELLY E. J.	PUTMAN J.
LAMBERT J. W.	RICHARDS J. A.
LARGIN J.	ROBERTSON S. T.
LAWLOR A. A.	ROOS R. A.
LAWRENCE V. S.	SELL H. T.
LENNARD J. A.	SHERMAN L.
LOCK L. O.	SMITH F. N.
LOCKHART N.	SMITH J.
McCARTHY B. J.	SMITH R. H.
McCLIFTY D.	SMITH W. S.
McDONALD A.	WHITEMAN H. J.
McLEOD K.	WILLIAMS A. A.
McRAE K.	WILSON E. C.

INF.

34TH BN. AUSTRALIAN I

longer missing'. Standing by the Australian section at the Menin Gate, it was on seeing those names that it affected her. She speaks of her granddad who survived the war; he signed up too young, lying about his age. There is also a story in her family that a 'great-uncle Hubert' died in the Somme – but it's not clear whether he was a real uncle as she has not found any trace of him on the family tree.

Ant – school student

Ant says at first that he didn't have any particular thoughts or feelings when the body was found, but then says: 'I would like to find his age. ... It was amazing how many people it takes to excavate a body. ... It would have got to me more if the skull was there.'

Steve – policeman

Steve explains that when he was excavating an Argyle & Sutherland Highlander's body (at Auchy on the Loos battlefield in Spring 2008), 'my feeling was to do my best for him: once you start you must finish' (talking about excavating and exhuming the body properly and ensuring all his belongings are recovered). In our discussions on the rights and wrongs of excavating bodies he says, 'Don't you want to put him back with his mates?'

Carl – retired banker

This is Carl's first time on a dig. On the afternoon the body is found, he comments that it's very poignant to find a body and mentions the families who might have a missing relative and what it would mean to them to have the body returned.

Commissaire de Police
(and younger policeman in charge of these finds at Commissariat at Comines)

Commissaire: He speaks of 'respect for the remains [respet des dépouilles]' as the reason for exhuming properly and carefully. He says that Belgians and English are very sensitive to this, while the French less so. He tells us that the police have to be super-careful with people finding bodies because of the 'amateurs' who find a body and show no respect for the remains as they look for artefacts to rob, and alludes to 'a case even here locally'. Also,

personal effects must be scrutinised to make sure it's really a corpse from the war. The younger policeman says that it's not a problem when a few bones are found but when it's a whole body there's an issue of respect for the remains as well as the possibility that it's a more recent/non-war related corpse. He is emphatic about the fact that in Belgium it's the state that is responsible for military bodies, through the Army: 'They say it's the Commonwealth [War Graves Commission] but it's the Belgian state.'

Michel Delrue – farmer

Standing by the trench where the body has been found a few hours ago Michel comments: 'It does something to us, to see this. It was someone's child.' He says that in the past it wasn't like that, they weren't sensitive to this; just after the war they found them 'just like that' and didn't necessarily retrieve them. He feels it's 'logical' that things should have changed. Now people are interested. He has found three bodies in one of his fields, and two Germans were identified.

Michel and Jeanne Delrue – farmers

The finding of the body led to another, longer conversation with both of the current landowners that reveals further their own attitude, as local residents, to such finds. They ask about the possibility of identification and express empathy with the soldier's family, happy that the soldier has been found and will be properly buried. However, they also add that until recently the view both of residents and local authorities would have been to leave the remains where they were found, so as to avoid problems: "They would say, just leave them where they are, that's their cemetery." People in the area have been used to coming across soldiers' remains ever since the war, and the 'change of mentality' has only come in this past generation, firstly by the changing attitudes of the authorities – particularly influenced by the example of the British operating in the area and their concern with identifying and reburying – and, secondly, to the fact that the war's survivors found bones all the time. 'At first there were bones every day, bits of bones were collected with the potatoes and discarded with the stones, or a hole dug and they were put back in.' It was not just familiarity, but also that people had been brutalised by the events, rendered insensitive to such finds by the sheer number of dead they had encountered: 'They had seen such massacres, such tragedies; all they had seen were dead bodies upon dead bodies.' Emerging from a destructive war meant that they had other worries, first and foremost making ends meet: "They must work every day of the week, morning to evening, just to feed themselves. They didn't think about anything else." It is only now, when people have leisure and the war is receding into the past, that sensitivities are changing. The rescue of such remains is also a way to teach the young about history.

Swantje – forensic archaeologist

The Plugstreet Project was a very good opportunity for me as a forensic and biological anthropology student to gain some experience in the field of battlefield archaeology, in this case regarding the First World War. It was my first proper field experience and I did learn a lot about history and archaeology. We were digging up trenches and found things like fabrics, bullet cases, tins, and bottles. We were also looking for human remains, as one year before two skeletons from soldiers were found and identified as Germans. A fundamental part of my work is the examination of skeletal material from once-living humans. I was asked on the site on several occasions how I would feel if we found a German soldier. My response would be that the nationality of a soldier does not personally matter to me. All and every remnant of a soldier would be treated with care and respect and therefore with an appropriate dignity, without any exception. Fact is, these men died too early and too young under conditions of war that are hard to imagine, caused by political decisions. Although the museums around Ypres are trying to describe the picture of the war, it was and still is, difficult to imagine the horror and terror the soldiers had to endure.

We saw pictures of the site, how it used to look during the war and we learned

that the ponds were craters and the results of massive mine explosions in 1917. Thousands of soldiers lost their lives in these fields and it again shows how senseless war is and how much potential is lost with every day of a fight. Working on this project was and still is learning more about the past, and maybe at some point being able to give a soldier a name and send him back home, in order to give him a decent burial and possibly provide closure to his existing families and relatives.

A First World War living history re-enactment group stopped by the site and showed us the uniforms and equipments of the soldiers. We therefore got an idea of what we could find during the excavation. Also, visits to surrounding museums gave us an insight of the time and what had happened in Ypres and specifically at the site of the excavation. Of particular interest was reading and learning about the Christmas Truce, which happened on a field next to the excavation side. Over a few days the soldiers stopped fighting. They exchanged cigarettes, tins and other things instead and showed each other photographs of their beloved ones. It makes one wonder what would have happened if the peace of Christmas 1914 had lasted, but the generals and politicians had other aims in their minds. There are, and perhaps always have been, atrocities in this world that we should never forget or deny. But it seems that some people need to be reminded that there is not only the past, but also the present.

When Data Are Human

The humanising of the soldier's remains has also been reinforced by the responses in Australia to his discovery. No sooner had the news of our work reached the Australian media than the Australian War Memorial began to receive requests for more information from the descendants of men still missing at Messines. Although some could be discounted because they were men recovered, reburied on the field and then lost in the confusion of war, others may yet prove to be worthy of further research. This Australian attachment to their dead was already well known to the excavators, including one of the team who had worked on the site at Fromelles, where a political campaign in Australia had led to the investigation of a previously unexplored mass grave from 1916. On a much more personal level, one grave in Toronto Avenue had been visited in the days before the dig started in 2008. The visitors had left a postcard of the town from which they and their ancestor had come. Sealed in with the card was a leaf from an Australian tree – perhaps one that grew on family land – which would have been known to both soldier and those paying their respects so many years later.

The Artist's Eye

While the process of excavation continued, Dr Peter Chasseaud was walking the landscape, considering the ground on and around the site. Peter has a dual role in the project, as both landscape archaeologist and as artist in residence. Here he presents his thoughts from the latter perspective:

I have been working on aspects of landscape (including artwork, text and poetry) at St Yvon with the No Man's Land team for two years. My approach to landscape, developed over a lifetime as an artist and writer, as well as an historian of maps, aerial photography and intelligence, has led me to believe in the necessity for a holistic and phenomenological approach to appearance and reality, in which I experience the place, and encounter, interrogate and understand the landscape, through a fusion of multi-aspect research with data acquired through walking, looking and feeling – indeed, using all my senses.

My approaches to observing the landscape (and looking at air photos) depend upon letting the landscape, or its image, speak to me, an approach which may appear passive, but which is deeply processual and informed. My method involves deliberate searching for and analysis of, objects, features, patterns, structures, indications, clues.

Landscape is a human construction, a text which can be read. It is a landscape of people and their history – created by people over millennia. It is Landscape of conflict. It is a landscape of current agricultural, economic and social activity. It is a landscape of memory, of remembrance and of tourism.

Many of the conflict landscape elements are invisible, but the informed mind envisions the phenomena beneath the surface. What is this landscape which we cannot see? Scratch the ground and find the trenches, pill-boxes, rusted detritus of conflict, human remains. Scrape the earth from the bones, the meat-paste jars, the mineral-water bottles. The trenches and whatever was deposited in them are below the surface – that is to say, their material remains in the form of rotting timbers, rusty corrugated iron, steel pickets and barbed wire, corroded munitions,

ABOVE *Martin Brown discusses progress with project cartographer and artist, Peter Chasseaud.*

LEFT *Peter Chasseaud's painting of one of the many pollarded willows in the Wallonian landscape.*

LEFT BOTTOM *One of the Messines attack mine craters.* Peter Chasseaud

etc. Those parts which were above ground (massive sandbag breastworks some 6ft high and 20ft thick, sometimes containing concrete pill-boxes, in the case of the Germans) were flattened and removed in a massive clearance operation after 1918.

I like the way the archaeologists look at the landscape and the ground. They are like artists in that they really observe; they imagine what might be, they think about what they see. Cutting a section, they see where a slight change in soil colour and/ or texture reveals the outline of a shell-hole or trench. They see the thin line of different-coloured material that separates two strata, that distinguishes the later fill from the earlier trench, the trench from the original undisturbed clay soil. So much of their work is about looking. Much is about surveying and drawing. These are all related activities involving sight. Technology aids this – photography, geophysics. The latter creates an image of what is beneath the surface – seeing beneath our feet.

Some of my landscape drawings are deliberately in the style of panorama drawings of the war period. I survey the landscape carefully. I select what to include and what to exclude. I measure bearings to key points, reference points. I mark these on the drawing. Later I can compare these drawings with both drawn and photographic panoramas made during the war, and see how the landscape has changed.

Some drawings are acts of imagination. I drew in pencil the view from the old British front line (Trench 123) looking across no-man's-land to the present wood and the trees around Factory Farm where the German front line once ran. I carefully marked the positions of the mine craters, and then began to transform the image. Using charcoal and white pastel, I inverted the light values to make night of day, and

RIGHT *Peter conducts a topographic survey in much the same manner as artillerymen of the Great War, noting particular landscape features which were essential for successfully ranging target fire.*

at the same time imagined the great pillars of fire shooting up from the huge mines laid at a depth of some 25m from the Trench 122 shaft and galleries. I showed the light of the explosions flooding no-man's-land, and silhouetting the barbed-wire entanglements. What I did not show was the simultaneous deaths of the Bavarian troops, the defenders of the trenches and strongpoints here, who were blown into the air, crushed to pulp, buried alive beneath the falling debris. Nor the deaths of the Australians of the 33rd Battalion who died in the assault and subsequent consolidation of the Ultimo crater.

Yet my other influences include the willow trees, such a predominant feature of the Flanders landscape, and their remains and shadows. They have regenerated from ancient willows which, after being whittled down by three years of British shellfire, were blasted by a stupendous mine explosion, buried under the debris of blue clay and yellow sand, brick, steel girders and concrete lumps of the German concrete strongpoints and shelters.

Thinking Local

There is undeniable local interest in the project, as visitors to the site show, but this is particularly demonstrated at the Ploegsteert Memorial to the missing, where once a month the local Memorial Committee organises a Last Post ceremony with wreath-laying and silence. This is not a recent attempt to mimic the more famous ceremony held each night at the Menin Gate in Ypres. It is actually the revival of a ceremony held in the inter-war years. Belgian veterans and police, local people and even residents of the local care home attend. It doesn't matter that the number of British visitors is few; this is about the Belgians and the fallen. After 90 years there is still a sense of honour.

At the same time the Belgians continue to live in the region and recognise that it has what might be termed a 'unique selling point' through its particular First World War history and associations. Mixed with the honour they accord the soldiers is a pragmatic sense of business; in an area where jobs are not plentiful outside farming it makes sense to develop interest in visiting the region. To this end the Plugstreet Project has been happy to liaise with one body who are developing a museum near the memorial that will look at the region in the war, including both military and civilian stories. Meanwhile, a proposed network of independent auberges offering good local food (what might be termed gastro-pubs in Britain) also encompasses the conflict heritage as one of the reasons for visiting Wallonia. Most locally, Claude, chef-patron of the Auberge opposite the Memorial, offers cuvée Ploegsteert wine, which features the memorial on its label, not only adopting the landmark but associating itself with various meanings that ensure sales to battlefield tourists.

While the Front is a landscape of memory, a vast cemetery, a former battlefield with live munitions, it is important to remember that it continues as a living, community-based landscape. If some locals are slightly bemused by our interest, others recognise the historical facts of the war and its continuing legacy and are prepared to work with both us and it. We may have our perspectives and opinions, but it remains their land, one which is still recovering from the events we study.

Wider Perspectives

We believe that it is a privilege to excavate in someone else's country on a site of international cultural significance. Locally, we have engaged with the Comines-Warneton Historical Society and have welcomed their members as volunteers and observers to the excavation. In addition, with them, we hold a news conference each year to present our findings to the local media and we have deliberately made this a common story of European history, ensuring as much weight is given to the Belgian narratives as to those of the soldiers. Meanwhile, the site blog[1] was set up to allow remote access to the dig and to keep interested people up to date between digging seasons. The team have also been encouraged to add contributions to the blog and have reflected both the scientific and social side of the project. Entries have been written in UK, American and Australian English, German, and even Basque, reflecting the international composition of the team. Finally, scientific reports have been composed in both English and French, including contributions for the region's *Chroniques de l'Archaeologie*, which present annual summaries of research in Wallonia. It is our contention that this is a global event and, as such, our perspectives need to be wider than the trenches, the Australians or the men in uniform. The scale of events behoves us to bring the widest range of techniques and perspectives possible: the scientific, intuitive, experiential and subjective. Total war requires total archaeology!

Thinking about the battlefield

The Western Front is a symbolic landscape for our time. After 90 years, it remains a testament to, and a metaphor for, the defining human invention of the 20th century – industrialised war. Since 1914, the Western Front in Belgium and France has become a concept

as well as a legacy of conflict – its multiple landscapes composed of a complex layering of human actions, experiences, emotions, and memories that have mingled with the physical remains of war. Although the Ypres salient in Belgium and the Somme in France have dominated perceptions of First World War conflict landscapes, many other sites of epic struggle exist. One of these is the area in western Belgium known as Ploegsteert-St Yvon ('Plugstreet' to the anglophone Allies) – the scene of bitter fighting in 1917, and, memorably, of the detonating of 19 Allied mines beneath German front lines on the morning of 7 June of that year.

Making places – Nick Saunders

Anthropologists and archaeologists do not see conflict landscapes as empty backgrounds to war, nor do they regard them simply as fossilised remnants of battle. They see these landscapes as pro-active, stationary yet ever-

BELOW *With Messines in the background on its prominent ridge, local children visit the excavations at st Yvon.*

RIGHT *A close-up on the metal plate on the front of the Pickelhaube found with the Australian. The lion rampant holding a sword is the emblem of Hesse.*

BELOW *Derek Smith records the excavation work to the British blockhouse and trenches at St Yvon.*

changing, full of memories as well as human bodies and the detritus of war, and open to many kinds of interpretation. To investigate such places, the Plugstreet Project draws on the wealth of knowledge gained not just by archaeology and anthropology, but also geography, military history, cultural history, and those whose expertise lies in tourism, heritage, and museums. This unique synthesis offers a powerful hybrid approach to the multi-layered reality of battlefield landscapes.

Ploegsteert-St Yvon is simultaneously an agricultural landscape, an industrialised slaughter house, a tomb for 'the missing', a place for returning refugees, a tourist destination, a location of memorials and pilgrimage, a site for archaeological research, cultural heritage development and television documentaries, and, of course, a still deadly place full of unexploded shells and bombs. Modern archaeological research seeks to figuratively unpack each of these landscapes, to recognise them as being ways in which different people engage with the region, and thereby to acknowledge, interpret, and preserve the various juxtaposed histories of the area. These battle-zone landscapes are as 'socially constructed' as they are technologically created by four years of industrialised war.

The First World War in this area destroyed a largely medieval landscape, finely balanced between architectural splendour and such rural features as the sophisticated medieval drainage systems, field boundaries, coppices, and moated farms. This landscape became a factory of industrialised death – 'drenched with hot metal', cut by trenches, undercut by mining tunnels, swathed in barbed wire, poisoned with gas, soaked with human blood, and disfigured by blasted trees and shell-craters. At the Factory Farm site of Ploegsteert-St Yvon, an upturned German bunker now sits just below the water level of the flooded mine crater blown on 7 June 1917. The crater is fringed by willows and, nearby, the modern fields are defined by post-1918 boundary ditches that in fact are a testament to a re-emergent medieval landscape.

The physical and psychological intensities of this destruction created a new and very different world for soldiers – a universe of trenches, dugouts, deafening artillery bombardments, and blind advances across no-man's-land. As the human body is our way of relating to and perceiving the world, it is not surprising that the shattering of people and terrain fragmented reality for the soldiers who fought here. This was a short-lived world of different sensibilities – a landscape of terrifying personal experiences only occasionally glimpsed today in diaries, war poetry, and battlefield remains.

Meaningful places

Landscapes themselves are artefacts, and possess an ambiguous relationship with other artefacts that represent them – particularly small objects that can appear as museum exhibits, souvenirs, or miscellaneous items found with human remains – and are embodiments of, and material witnesses to, the human experience of war.

Two examples illustrate the point. Rifleman Vincent Sabini of 18th Battalion, 'London Irish' Regiment, 47th London Division, went over the top at Messines on 7 June 1917, just a few kilometres from St Yvon. Hit in the knee by a German bullet, he was hospitalised in England. When he recovered, he fashioned a crucifix from the bullet removed from his body, and wore it around his neck until his death in 1981 aged 90. Through painful wounding, impaired walking, and physical adornment, the bullet had re-made Sabini's private and public body, first at Messines, then at home in England. This relationship between body, bullet, crucifix and landscape was perpetuated by Sabini's nephew, Tony Spagnoly, who inherited the item. A well-known First World War battlefield historian and tour guide, he wore the crucifix until his own death in 2008, and was buried still wearing it.

An anonymous Australian soldier of 33rd Battalion, Australian 3rd Division, was discovered during excavations near to the Ultimo crater at Ploegsteert-St Yvon in August 2008. No crucifix was found, but several items did open the door to the dead soldier's social world from 1917. Among his possessions was found a German pickelhaube helmet – a popular souvenir with Allied soldiers. While it is possible that he picked it up in the German front-line trench as he passed through, more likely he acquired it as a war souvenir en route to the Front. Equally insightful is an altered copper bullet casing that may have served as an amuletic charm, in a not dissimilar fashion to Sabini's bullet crucifix. Both items immediately humanised the skeletal remains, connecting the soldier to the world of souvenir collecting during the war, and the battlefield superstitions that attached themselves to men about to face death. These objects located the man in social landscapes, and demonstrated the transformative power of material culture in a terrain itself an artefact of war.

Vincent Sabini and the anonymous Australian were casualties of the opening moments of the Battle of Messines and both, in different ways, have had their humanity preserved and transformed by the objects of war. Tracing these items across time and space, creates biographies of the objects and the men, fixes them in a place in the landscape, speaks to their social relationships and identities, and gives a poignant voice to one man whose life was ended, and another whose life was forever changed.

The Plugstreet Project's focus on landscape at Ploegsteert-St Yvon has shown, even at this early stage, that this under-investigated part of the Western Front conceals a rich palimpsest of knowledge about and insight into the human experience of war and its legacies. Landscapes are made by and for people, and this area today still conceals many of those who created it between 1914 and 1918. Here, literally and symbolically, human beings and landscape have become one.

At the Going Down of the Sun

Perhaps the successes of the 1917 Battle of Messines have been overshadowed by the third Battle of Ypres, to which the attack has become viewed as a prelude. Perhaps the limited objectives of 'bite and hold' have meant that it is a battle less well known than others. In some ways it might simply be that this battle does not fit in with the general picture of the futile war of châteaux-bound commanders sending teenaged soldiers to brutal butchery.

What can be said is that this campaign is one that deserves greater study, Ian Passingham's splendid work notwithstanding.[2]

This was the first 'all-arms' battle of modern war, with tanks, artillery, air cover and infantry all working in a carefully co-ordinated plan. It also shows how intricate training was accomplished and led to the successes, enabling troops to adapt to their conditions and show versatility when faced with unusual situations. At St Yvon, the attacking Allied soldiers accomplished their aim to turn the enemy positions around. They cut firesteps where this was possible, but were still able to make new positions from corrugated iron where it was not. The training was also effective in ensuring that crater defences were created swiftly, essential to the success of the operation. Messines shows that the overall Allied High Command had learned the lessons of previous campaigns.

The excavations at St Yvon have highlighted all this, alongside illustrating how men lived in these trenches and how they died from bullet, shell and mine blast. Although bodies are often discovered by farmers who work the reclaimed land, archaeological treatment of human remains is essential in gaining as much information as possible to ascertain an identity for the individual and to end with a name inscribed on the man's headstone rather than simply his evocation as being 'known unto God'.

This battle has perhaps a unique resource with all the documents available in the UK and Australia, as well as the surviving physical traces – be they mine craters, trenches, graffiti on trees, or bunkers – relating to a short, specific battle which moved the Front forwards. It is crucial that archaeological work on First World War sites should be multifaceted, with art anthropology, photography, memory, empathy and emotion. There is much work that remains to be done, but it must be done properly.

First World War archaeology, although new, is an essential element of study. The Plugstreet Project has aimed to follow a single unit from their training through to the maelstrom of the Western Front, but is it much more than that; it discusses the greater whole. It has highlighted that, although a landscape may seem utterly destroyed, pulverised, it can still hold memory and information. It has been a privilege to work in Wallonia, to work with local people and listen to their stories; to highlight the role of training in the First World War; and to recover the unknown Australian. The work of the team does not occur in a vacuum; given the close proximity of the conflict, we all have our family connections and this thus becomes an act of remembrance as well as research.

Our studies have thus shown that this war's archaeology extends far beyond 'digging trenches'; we are able to gain so much more from a multi-disciplinary approach. Ours is a story of those men that trained, fought, and in many cases died, in a short period of time. The First World War did not take place in isolation on a blank canvas of untouched landscape; it is also a tale of the land that was fought over, and Belgians who were forced to leave and then had to try to restore what was left of their world following the armistice.

Our battle is a microcosm of the First World War itself, the phenomenon of the missing. As such it also looks at the individual soldier, and becomes the narrative of the poor bloody infantry whose tale is too often ignored in favour of discussions of regiments, of battles, of commanders. As one British infantryman who fought in the Napoleonic Wars, Private Wheeler, once said:

I have often been tickled on reading the General despatches of the Army, when some Lord or General or Colonel has been killed or wounded. Fame takes her trumpet and sounds it through the world ... then follows a long lamentation. ... But who shall record the glorious deeds of the soldier whose lot is numbered with the thousands in the ranks who live and die and fight in obscurity.[3]

Perhaps it is archaeology that can best attest to these deeds.

1 <http://www.plugstreet.blogspot.com>.
2 Passingham, 2004.
3 Liddell Hart (ed.), 1951.

BELOW *All the excavation team in front of the Ploegsteert Memorial at the end of the excavation in 2007.*

Bibliography and Sources

Anon, *Where the Australians Rest – a description of the Cemeteries overseas in which Australians including those whose names can never now be known are buried* (Government Printer, Melbourne, 1920)

Barton, P., Doyle, P., and Vandewalle, J., *Beneath Flanders Fields – the Tunnellers' War 1914-18* (Staplehurst, Spellmount, 2004)

Bean, C.E.W., *The Australian Imperial Force in France 1917* (Angus and Robertson, 1943)

Bostyn, F., Blieck, K., Declerck, F., Descamps, F., and Van der Fraenen, J., *Passchendaele 1917: the Story of the Fallen and Tyne Cot Cemetery* (Barnsley, Pen and Sword, 2007)

Bourgeois, H., 'Le problème de la reconstruction provisoire à Comines-Belgiques, Houtern et Bas-Warneton après la Grande Guerre', Mémoires de la Société d'Histoire de Comines-Warneton et de la Région, t. VIII, fasc. 2 (1978), 367–98

Bourgeois, J., 'Les Sites Fossoyes Medievaux a Comines-Warneton: Synthese', Memoires de la Societe d'Histoire de Comines-Warneton, 33 (2003), 15–32

——, 'Les Sites Fossoyes Medievaux de la Region de Comines-Warneton (Province de Hainaut Belgique)', *Revue du Nord*, 85 (2003), 141–59

Carnel, S., *La Reconstruction des Régions Dévastées après la Première Guerre Mondiale: le cas de Neuve-Église*, Société d'Histoire de Comines-Warneton et de la Région (Comines-Warneton, 2002)

Chasseaud, P., *Rats Alley: Trench Names of the Western Front 1914–18* (Stroud, Spellmount, 2006)

Chielens, P., Dendooven, D., and Decoodt, H., *De Laatste Getuige* (Tielt, Lannoo, 2006)

Clout, H., *After the Ruins: Restoring the Countryside of Northern France after the Great War* (Exeter, University of Exeter Press, 1996)

Cobb, R., *French and Germans, Germans and French: a Personal Interpretation of France under Two Occupations, 1914–1918/1940–1945* (Hanover and London, University Press of New England, 1983)

Conan Doyle, A., *Sherlock Holmes: the Complete Illustrated Novels* (London, Chancellor Press, 1993; 1st pub. 1890)

Cuttriss, G.P., *Over the Top with the 3rd Australian Division* (1918)

Desfosses Y., Jacques, A., and Prilaux, G., *L'archaeologie de la Grande Guerre* (Rennes: Editions Ouest France/Inrap, 2008)

Doyle, P., *Tommy's War, British Military Memorabilia* (Crowood, Ramsbury, 2008)

Edwards, J., *Never a Backwards Step: a History of the First 33rd Battalion AIF* (Grafton, New South Wales, Beetong Books, 1996)

Fairey, E., *The 38th Battalion A.I.F.: the Story and Official History of the 38th Battalion A.I.F.* (Bendigo, 38th Battalion History Committee, 1920)

Holmes, R., *Tommy: the British Soldier on the Western Front 1914–1918* (London, Harper Collins, 2004)

Jones, D., *Bullets and Bandsmen* (Salisbury, Owl, 1992)

Keatinge, M.B.B., *War Book of the Third Pioneer Battalion. Compiled by M.B.B. Keatinge and a Committee of the Battalion* (Melbourne, Specialty Press, 1922)

Laffin, J., *Digging Up the Diggers' War: Australian Battlefield Archaeology* (Kenthurst, New South Wales, Kangaroo Press, 1993)

Liddell Hart, B. (ed.), *The Letters of Private Wheeler* (London, Michael Joseph, 1951)

MacDonald, L., *1915: The Death of Innocence* (London, Headline, 1993)

McNicoll, N.G., *The Thirty-Seventh: History of the 37th Battalion A.I.F.* (Melbourne, Modern Printing Company, 1936)

McPhail, H., *The Long Silence: Civilian Life under the German Occupation of Northern France, 1914–1918* (London and New York, I.B. Tauris Publishers, 2001)

Molkentin, M., *Training for War: The Third Division A.I.F. at Lark Hill*, 1916 (2005, unpublished)

——, *Trench Warfare 101: Training at the Bustard Trenches, Wartime* (Journal of the Australian War Memorial), 33 (2006), 48–50.

Moran, C. M., *The Anatomy of Courage* (London, Robinson, 2007; 1st pub. 1945)

Nivet, P., *Les Réfugiés Français de la Grande Guerre (1914–1920)*: les 'Boches du Nord' (Paris, Economica, 2004)

O'Brien, T., *The Things They Carried* (London, Flamingo, 1990)

Osgood, R., and Brown, M., *Au champ d'honneur . . . Recherche archéologique à Comines-Warneton*, été 2007 Les Cahiers de l'Urbanisme No 65 (September 2007)

——, Brown, M., and Hawkins, L., *Before the Storm: The Australian 3rd Division on Salisbury Plain in the First World War, Wartime* (Journal of the Australian War Memorial), 34 (2006)

Palazzo, A., *Defenders of Australia: the Third Australian Division, 1916–1991* (Canberra, Army History Unit, Department of Defence, 2002)

Parez, R., 'Le problème de la reconstruction de Warneton après la guerre de 1914–1918 et la vie des rapatriés', Mémoires de la Société d'Histoire de Comines-Warneton et de la Région, t. VIII, fasc. 2 (1978), 399–460

Passingham, I., *Pillars of Fire – The Battle of Messines Ridge, June 1917* (Stroud, Sutton Publishing, 2004)

Pedersen, P., *The Anzacs: Gallipoli to the Western Front*, (Camberwell, Australia, Viking (Penguin), 2007)

Reconstructions, *Reconstructions en Picardie après 1918*, (Paris, Éditions de la Réunion des Musées Nationaux, 2000)

Reed, P., *Walking the Salient* (Barnsley, Pen & Sword, 2001)

Roelens, P. and Bril, E., *Découverte des corps de deux soldats allemands de la première guerre mondiale*, Mémoires de la Société d'Histoire de Comines-Warneton et de la Région, 36 (2006 (a)), 263–6

——, and Bril, E., *Découverte des corps de trois soldats anglais de la première guerre mondiale à Warneton*, Mémoires de la Société d'Histoire de Comines-Warneton et de la Région, 36 (2006 (b)), 267–72

The 7th Field Artillery Brigade, *The Yandoo*, containing publications of the organ of the 7th Field Artillery Brigade, Australian Imperial Forces, while in camp at various artillery training centres in the south of England, principally at Lark Hill, Salisbury Plain, (7th Field Artillery Brigade, *The Yandoo*, vol II, part 5, 20 November 1916, unpublished)

Saunders, N.J., *Trench Art: Materialities and Memories of War* (Oxford, Berg, 2003)

——, *Killing Time: Archaeology and the First World War* (Stroud, Sutton Publishing, 2007)

Sheldon, J., *The German Army at Passchendale* (Barnsley, Pen & Sword, 2007)

Simkins, P., *Kitchener's Army* (Barnsley, Pen & Sword, 2007)

Spagnoly, T. and Smith, T., *Cameos of the Western Front – a Walk Round Plugstreet*, (Barnsley, Pen and Sword, 2003)

Swift, E., *Where they Lay: the Search for Those who Fell in Battle and were Left Behind* (London, Bantam Press, 2003)

Todman, D., *The Great War, Myth and Memory* (London, Hambledon & London, 2005)

Van der Meersch, M., *Invasion 14* (Paris, Albin Michel, 1935)

Vegetius [390], De Re Militari (1767)
    <http://www.pvv.ntnu.no/~madsb/home/war/vegetius/>

Wallace,J., *Digging the Dirt* (London, Duckworth, 2004)

Walle, J.-C., 'Au lendemain de la guerre de 1914–1918 Ploegsteert renait de ses cendres', Mémoires de la Société d'Histoire de Comines-Warneton et de la Région, t. VIII, fasc. 2 (1978), 460–86

War Office, *Field Service Pocket Book* (London, HMSO, 1917)

War Office, *Manual of Field Works (All Arms)* (London, HMSO, 1921)

Wyeth, R., *Warriors for the Working Day: Codford during Two World Wars* (Salisbury, Hobnob Press, 2002)

<http://www.awm.gov.au/cms_images/AWM4/23/AWM4-23-50-8.pdf>, AWM4 Australian Imperial Force Unit War Diaries, 1914–18 War, Infantry, Item No 23/50/8, 33rd Infantry Battalion, June 1917

Index